The Winter's Tale

WILLIAM SHAKESPEARE

Guide written by

Sandra Langdon

A *Letts* Literature Guide

First published 1997

Letts Educational
Aldine House
Aldine Place
London W12 8AW
0181 740 2266

Text © Sandra Langdon 1997

Typeset by Jordan Publishing Design

Text design Jonathan Barnard

Cover and text illustrations Hugh Marshall

Graphic illustration Hugh Marshall

Design © BPP (Letts Educational) Ltd

British Library Cataloguing in Publication Data
A CIP record for this book is available from the British Library

ISBN 1 85758 494 5

Printed and bound in Great Britain
by Nuffield Press, Abingdon

Letts Educational is the trading name of BPP (Letts Educational) Ltd

Contents

■ Plot synopsis

Polixenes, King of Bohemia, has been enjoying a long visit at the home of his childhood friend, Leontes, King of Sicilia. Polixenes announces that he must return home, but Leontes insists that he stay another week. When Leontes cannot persuade Polixenes to extend his visit he asks his wife, Hermione, to try her charms on his friend. She is so successful that Leontes becomes insanely jealous and concludes that they have been having an affair. He orders his trusted lord, Camillo, to poison Polixenes, but instead Camillo warns Polixenes of Leontes' irrational turn and the two men escape from Sicilia secretly during the night.

Hermione and her ladies-in-waiting are being entertained by her son, Prince Mamillius. They are interrupted by Leontes who, upon hearing of Polixenes' and Camillo's sudden departure, is further convinced of the affair. He publicly accuses his wife of being an adulteress and of carrying Polixenes' child. He orders her to be imprisoned. The other lords speak in Hermione's defence, but he ignores their pleas, deciding instead to send two lords to Delphos in Greece to ask the Oracle of Apollo to judge the case.

The stress of the imprisonment and the accusations cause Hermione to go into premature labour and she gives birth to a daughter. Paulina, wife of Lord Antigonus, takes the baby to Leontes in the hopes that the sight of the innocent child will bring him back to his senses. Her plan backfires, however – believing the child to be a bastard, Leontes orders it to be burned to death. Antigonus and the other lords beg him to spare the child's life, and he relents, deciding instead that Antigonus will abandon the baby in a remote place, where its survival will be left up to fate.

The lords sent to Delphos return with the Oracle's judgement. Leontes calls for a Court of Justice to try Hermione. She is charged with high treason in committing adultery with Polixenes, conspiring with Camillo to kill Leontes and helping Polixenes and Camillo to escape. She pleads not guilty, and, when her self-defence has no effect, she asks for the Oracle's judgement to be read. The Oracle judges Hermione and Polixenes not guilty of adultery, the baby to be legitimate and Leontes to be a tyrant who will have no heir until the lost child is found. Leontes insists the judgement is false. Immediately, news of Mamillius' death is announced and Hermione faints. She is removed from the court and Paulina later says that she is dead. Leontes realises his terrible sin and asks for Apollo's forgiveness. He says he will dedicate the rest of his life to grieving for his dead wife and son.

Meanwhile, Antigonus has taken the baby to a deserted part of Bohemia. He has dreamt of Hermione, whose death, he believes, proves her guilt. He abandons the baby, leaving her with documents for identification and gold coins to pay for her upbringing. After Antigonus is killed by a bear, a shepherd discovers the baby. He and his son believe the baby to be a gift from fairies and agree to take her home with them, but to keep her true identity secret.

Time comes on stage as a character, to announce that sixteen years have passed and that the story will now focus on the lost baby, Perdita.

In Bohemia, Camillo wishes to return home. Polixenes tells him to forget Sicilia, as he is needed to help discover why Prince Florizel has been spending so much time at the cottage of an old shepherd. Camillo agrees to Polixenes' plan to disguise themselves and pay the old shepherd a visit.

Perdita has grown into a beautiful young woman and is queen of the sheep-shearing festival. She and Florizel have fallen in love. Polixenes and Camillo arrive in disguise and talk to the young couple, and Florizel announces that he wishes to marry Perdita. Enraged, Polixenes reveals his identity and forbids the marriage. Before he leaves, he threatens Perdita with death if she tries to see Florizel again. Florizel denounces his father and the throne of Bohemia in favour of marrying Perdita. Camillo suggests that they go to Sicilia, where they will be welcomed by Leontes. Knowing that Polixenes will insist that they follow the couple, Camillo tells him where they have gone so that he will be able to return to Sicilia.

The old shepherd and his son are frightened by Polixenes' threats and decide to show him Perdita's identification documents. They are met on their way to the court by the thief, Autolycus, who misdirects them to the boat for Sicilia.

Leontes' welcome to the young couple is interrupted by a messenger from Polixenes, insisting that they are detained until his arrival. The old shepherd arrives at the court of Sicilia and reveals Perdita's identity. The couple's engagement is blessed by Polixenes, the kings are reconciled and Paulina learns of Antigonus' death. Following the revelations, the royal courts of the two countries go to Paulina's house for the unveiling of a statue of Hermione. Leontes is mesmerised by the statue and goes into a trance of repentance. The 'statue' moves off its stand towards Leontes, revealing itself to be Hermione, still alive. She has survived all these years in the hope of seeing the prophecy fulfilled. Delighted at being reunited with his wife, Leontes insists that Paulina marry Camillo. Everyone departs from Paulina's house to prepare for the two marriages.

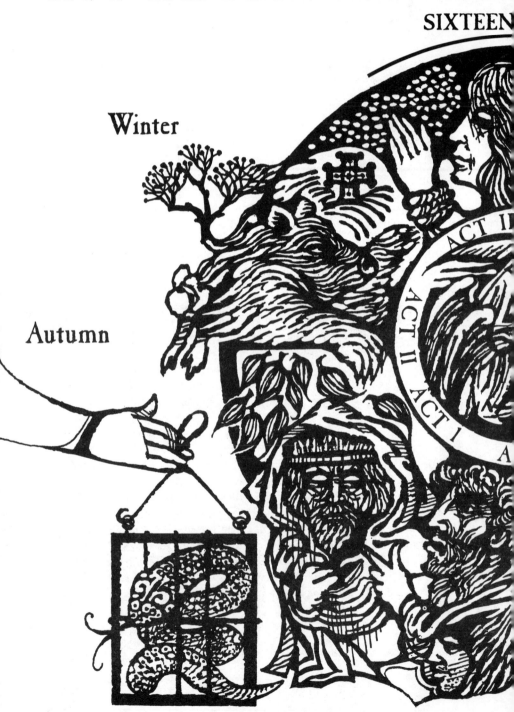

Winter

Autumn

ACT II

ACT I

ACT II ACT I A

THROUGH THE SEASONS

YEARS PASS

Spring

Summer

Leontes

Leontes

At the start of the play Leontes is a happily married, well-loved and well-respected man and doting father. So far his life has never known sin. His jealousy is unexpected and has no motive other than his hurt pride. Perhaps he was merely being frivolous in asking Hermione to talk Polixenes out of returning to Bohemia. Whether he was serious or not, he never expected her to be successful. His friendship with Polixenes meant a great deal to him and he took Polixenes at his word when he rejected Leontes' plea to stay.

The Winter's Tale is not concerned with the psychological origins of jealousy, but rather with its destructive consequences. Leontes' suspicion is irrational. In the first three acts of the play, it causes increasing destruction, climaxing in Leontes being branded as a tyrant by both Paulina and the Oracle's judgement in Act 3, scene 2.

Leontes represents man's capacity for destruction. His jealous fit becomes a consuming madness. Who else but a madman would reject the judgement of the Oracle? (People in Shakespeare's day believed devoutly in God as the supreme power. This play is set in pre-Christian times, but Shakespeare's audiences would recognise many of the religious and spiritual attitudes, such as the sin of showing hubris [extreme pride] before a divine power.) For someone to put himself above a divine power would definitely indicate madness, because it would be asking for divine punishment. Leontes is no exception and he is punished immediately by heaven after rejecting the Oracle. He destroys the lives of those around him, but ultimately his behaviour is self-destructive, as he loses his wife, son, faithful adviser and daughter, and alienates his closest friend.

Leontes' madness is reflected in his language and through imagery. His lines become harder to understand as his thinking becomes incoherent. Look at the punctuation of his lines during his reign of jealousy: what punctuation marks suggest that he is talking without thinking about what he is saying? Compare these lines to his words after his reason has been restored. The first half of the play contains many images of disease and decay, reinforcing the 'disease' in Leontes' mind.

However, Leontes' character also represents the powers of repentance and forgiveness. His grief gives way to regret and he spends the second half of the play repenting for his sins. We might question why he never searched for his lost child: perhaps he did not want to challenge the Oracle a second time. Act 5 presents a changed Leontes, who has learned humility, tolerance and generosity. He shows humility before Paulina, tolerance and generosity in helping Perdita and Florizel, and, through repentance, is reconciled with what he had lost.

Hermione

Hermione

Hermione is introduced as a dutiful, loyal wife and gracious hostess. She makes Polixenes feel welcome because he is her husband's close friend. Notice that when she speaks to Polixenes it is to find out more about Leontes' boyhood. This is certainly not the conversation of a woman having an affair! She cleverly persuades Polixenes to stay in order to please her husband.

She is unaware of Leontes' suspicions in Act 1 and continues in her insouciant manner with Mamillius and the ladies-in-waiting at the beginning of Act 2. When Leontes accuses her of being an adulteress, she thinks he is joking. When she realises that he is serious, her carefree demeanour changes to one of fortitude and we never again see the happy and lighthearted Hermione of the first scenes.

Hermione is well-respected and loved throughout the court. No-one other than Leontes doubts her innocence, and one by one others speak to Leontes on her behalf. She faces her imprisonment with fortitude and demonstrates great humility in leaving her fate to the grace of God. The charges and imprisonment, however, do take a toll on her and she gives birth prematurely. In court, she defends herself with dignity and courage. Her well-reasoned arguments pose a direct contrast to Leontes' unsound thinking. She selflessly puts her children first, saying that she is defending her honour before her life. She would sooner die than have her children grow up stained by her bad name.

We can only guess why Hermione lets the court think she is dead for sixteen years. What is important is the symbolism of her apparent death and resurrection. In mythological terms, Hermione symbolises the goddess Demeter. You should be able to read about Demeter in most collections of classical myths.

Perdita

Perdita

Perdita's name means 'lost girl', signifying the Oracle's judgement that 'the King shall live without an heir, if that which is lost be not found'. She is born into a destructive world but is brought up close to nature. She is symbolised by flowers and represents creation and rebirth, hence her many references to fertility. Her verse in Act 4 is clever and articulate, recalling her mother and in contrast to her father's former hysterics. Her beauty and dignified demeanour are described in terms of a goddess of nature, and symbolised in her role as queen of the sheep-shearing feast.

Perdita is a strong character with a great deal of common sense and good taste. Her strength is demonstrated by her reaction to Polixenes' threats. She is not afraid of him and disagrees with his judgement, but knows that Florizel is in danger and puts his future before her own wishes. She is prepared never to see him again and asks him to leave. When he chooses her love over his birthright, she knows the risks involved and bravely accepts them in order to be with Florizel. Her good taste prevents her from admiring artificiality or enjoying Autolycus' crude songs. In fact, she disapproves of Florizel's praises, as she feels that romantic exaggerations are insincere.

Despite her obvious differences from him, Perdita has always behaved as a dutiful and respectful daughter to Shepherd. When she is reunited with her real father, Leontes, and hears of her mother's untimely death, she cries, but soon recovers, accepting the situation and wanting only to see the statue of her mother. A less generous and mature person could easily have judged Leontes. Perdita is presented as an ideal of purity, innocence, beauty and the creative force of nature and human nature combined.

Paulina

Paulina

Paulina acts as the audience's mouthpiece, Leontes' conscience, the Oracle's implement and Hermione's restorer. She has a strong sense of right and wrong. She is shocked when Leontes rejects his own daughter and unashamedly voices her condemnation (and that of the audience) of his behaviour. In the next act, when Leontes rejects the Oracle's decision, she knows that Mamillius' death is retribution for Leontes' hubris. At this point she is even more outspoken in her denunciation of Leontes, asking sarcastically what punishment he has for her. However, she is quick to regain her sense of fairness when Leontes shows remorse at what he has done.

Paulina loves Hermione and tells Leontes she is dead in order to protect her. Being strong-willed, she manages to advise Leontes and protect Hermione at the same time. She does not forgive Leontes easily, however, and instead helps him to earn his repentance through acting as his conscience. When all his other courtiers are prepared to forgive him his sins against Hermione and encourage him to remarry, it is Paulina who, painfully, reminds him of his responsibility for his destructive deeds. Leontes respects Paulina's judgement and submits to her will.

Paulina never forgets the Oracle's judgement and keeps Hermione alive in the hope that it will one day be fulfilled. Perhaps she secretly hopes that the return of the lost child will also bring the return of her lost husband, Antigonus. When she learns of Perdita's true identity, she skilfully plans to restore Hermione to her family. During the viewing of the statue, Paulina behaves almost as a high priestess in purposely stirring Leontes' emotions. This climaxes in her illusion of seemingly bringing the statue back to life. Who do you think is the strongest female character in the play – Hermione, Perdita or Paulina?

Polixenes

Polixenes

At the beginning of the play, Polixenes is introduced as Leontes' lifelong friend. They have much in common. Polixenes is a gracious guest at first, courteous to Hermione and speaking fondly of Leontes. It is he, however, who makes the comment that starts all the trouble, when he says that Leontes is the only person who can move him. Leontes then becomes jealous when Hermione's words persuade Polixenes to stay.

Polixenes is perceptive and knows Leontes well, so he notices his friend's strange behaviour immediately. He is outraged when he hears that Leontes thinks he defiled Hermione, but he wisely chooses to leave immediately rather than confront his friend.

The wound of Leontes' betrayal runs deep and sixteen years later, although formally reconciled to him, Polixenes is still disturbed by the tragic events following his last visit. As Leontes atones for his sins, Polixenes reveals some flaws. He keeps his word to Camillo in taking good care of him in Bohemia, but is selfish in wanting Camillo to stay in Bohemia rather than return to Sicilia. He condones Florizel having an unchaste love affair with a shepherdess, but becomes tyrannical at the thought of Florizel marrying her. His fury and wrath recalls Leontes' jealous rage sixteen years earlier. Like his friend, his temper costs him his child.

Given the social norms of the day, Polixenes' wrath is understandable. Luckily, his threats are never followed up and he is quickly reconciled with his family. His own worries over, his brotherly love returns and he offers to share Leontes' grief at the unveiling of Hermione's statue.

Camillo

Camillo

Camillo begins the play by providing background information about Leontes and his friendship with Polixenes. His conversation with Archidamus sets the initial tone of the play as one of sentimentality and goodwill between the two kings. For the remainder of the play Camillo's function is to act successively as an advisor to Leontes, Polixenes and Florizel. He represents good judgement, in contrast to Leontes' and Polixenes' abuse of power.

Camillo is a good and honourable man and will risk his life in order to do what he believes is right. Camillo usually puts the well-being of others before himself – he agrees to Leontes' order to poison Polixenes if it will save Hermione's reputation, and he forsakes promotion and risks his own life to save Polixenes. When Leontes regains his reason, he realises that Camillo saved him from further sin in betraying his plans to murder Polixenes.

Camillo's only lapse into selfishness occurs when he betrays Florizel's plans to Polixenes in order to return to Sicilia. Luckily, this betrayal has beneficial consequences so that we, and Florizel, can forgive Camillo for putting his own needs first. At the end of the play he is rewarded for all his good deeds by his marriage to Paulina.

Florizel

Florizel

Florizel is presented as a type rather than an individual, and represents chivalry in the play. A tradition of 'courtly romances' existed in the Middle Ages, and Shakespeare and his contemporaries would have been familiar with these tales, in which a knight would suffer and be prepared to die for the love of his lady. Here, Florizel is prepared to forsake his father and the throne of Bohemia for the love of Perdita. Presumably this decision puts his life in danger from Polixenes. He values honour and religious faith and he treats Perdita with respect. In comparing Perdita's beauty to a list of beautiful things, in Act 4, scene 4, his behaviour is also typical of a Shakespearean lover. His characterisation is kept to a minimum to accentuate the focus on Perdita.

Florizel is first referred to in Act 1, when Polixenes describes how much he loves his young son. What expectations do we have of Florizel from his father's description? How does Florizel meet these expectations when we meet him sixteen years later in Act 4, scene 4? There are also obvious parallels with Prince Mamillius. Florizel, no doubt, represents the type of young man Mamillius would have grown to be had he lived. Together, he and Perdita represent the meeting of the best features of the pastoral and courtly worlds.

Time

Time personified announces the change of setting in time and place in the play. His presence marks the transition in atmosphere and ideas from tragedy and destruction to comedy, romance and rebirth. His monologue sums up the ideas of time explored in this play.

Autolycus

Autolycus is a common thief and pedlar. His importance in the play is threefold: he is a symbol, a character foil to Perdita and an important plot device.

Autolycus is necessary to the scenes set in the country to provide a balance between the idyllic and the realistic. His existence is purely physical and his lewd songs remind us of the physical and sexual rhythms running rife through the country. He adds local colour and spice to an otherwise idyllic world. His immoral livelihood and songs present a perfect contrast to the refined, gentle, innocent and highly moral Perdita.

Autolycus' main function in the plot is to be a believable person with whom Florizel can swap clothes. A thief would happily exchange his clothes for money. It is his love of money that leads him to fool Shepherd and Clown into boarding the boat for Sicilia. (It is necessary that Shepherd and Clown go to Sicilia, so Autolycus provides a believable reason.) His scenes also provide comic relief after the tragic first half of the play. Whilst his asking for forgiveness from Clown and the Prince is humorous, it also reinforces this theme – forgiveness is not restricted to the gentle classes.

Antigonus

Antigonus is a lord of Sicilia and Paulina's husband. He is not provoked by Leontes' insult that he cannot control his wife. In fact his marriage, as one of mutual respect and equality, reinforces Leontes' tyranny by contrast with it. He is a wise man and tries to warn Leontes of the consequences of burning the child to death. He succeeds in saving her life and is responsible for Perdita's 'kinder fate' of abandonment.

Antigonus takes Perdita to a deserted region of Bohemia. (He had already set sail by the time of her mother's trial, and did not hear the Oracle judge Hermione innocent.) He is wrong in thinking that Hermione's death, as suggested by her appearance in his dream, confirms her guilt. This error in judgement causes him to abandon the 'bastard' and thereby lose his own life as punishment for his involvement.

Antigonus' cruel death represents the power of divine retribution, but seems unfair given that he saved Perdita from being burned to death. Why is his death necessary to the plot?

Shepherd

Shepherd represents the common man. His character is a mixture of folly, superstition and goodness. His folly allows him to be tricked easily by Autolycus, to worry about himself more than Perdita after Polixenes' threats and to take pleasure in his new-found status at the end of the play. His superstition leads him to believe that Perdita was a gift from fairies and that he could lose the gift if he reveals her origins. These weaknesses are balanced by his good acts. He rescues Perdita from abandonment and encourages Clown, at the end of the play, to forgive Autolycus.

Shepherd fails to recognise Florizel as the prince and as a result gets angry with the young lovers when Florizel's identity is revealed. He is well aware of the social norms preventing the intermixing of nobility and peasantry. This does not, however, inhibit him from showing off his improved status at the end of the play. The many contradictions in Shepherd's personality create humour in the second half of the play.

Clown

Clown represents the simplicity of the country peasant. He is an easy target for Autolycus and spends most of the play following his father's orders. He is supposedly Perdita's brother, but the contrast between them highlights her refinement and sophistication. His simplicity provides much humour, especially in his scenes with Autolycus. His simplicity signifies an innocence different from that of Perdita. Her innocence represents spiritual purity, whereas Clown's innocence represents ignorance. He does, however, have a sense of decorum and buries Antigonus' half-eaten body to allow Antigonus some dignity in death. How does Clown's character add to the atmosphere of country life?

■ Themes and images in *The Winter's Tale*

Jealousy and sin

Jealousy and sin

Jealousy is the fear of losing a loved one or valued possession to a rival. Sin is the breaking of a religious belief. Although not one of the Seven Deadly Sins, jealousy is considered a dangerous and destructive emotion and in Shakespeare's time it would have been considered a sin to submit to such feelings. What religious principle does jealousy offend?

It is never made clear in the play whether it is set in Christian or pagan times, as there are references to both. In either case, any sin committed would result immediately in destruction, even death, and would later be punished by a higher power. The sense that Leontes' jealousy is wrong is reinforced in the many images of disease in the play. As soon as Hermione is imprisoned, Mamillius falls sick and Leontes is unable to sleep. Keep a lookout for these references as you read the play. This imagery is particular to the scenes in Sicilia, and surface even in the closing act to highlight how badly that country was infected by Leontes' poisoned mind. Leontes says of Florizel and Perdita's visit: 'Purge all infection from our air whilst you do climate here!' What does the imagery of Leontes' words suggest?

Elizabethan audiences would certainly have expected Leontes' jealousy to cause destruction and to be punished. His jealousy blinds him to reason, leading him to make destructive decisions that result in the loss of his family and close friend. Even the honourable Antigonus suffers death as punishment for his involvement in Leontes' evil deeds. What sin does Antigonus commit, allowing him to endorse Leontes' jealousy? Leontes' sixteen years of suffering for his sin would be deemed a more cruel punishment than his own death. He finds salvation through the processes of repentance, time, rebirth and forgiveness.

Repentance

Repentance

Repentance is the acknowledgement of suffering for a bad deed. The aim of repentance is to be forgiven by a spiritual power. Leontes repents for the deaths of Hermione and Mamillius by grieving for sixteen years. He lost his family through his sin of jealousy, which blinded him to reason and in turn resulted in his more serious sin of pride when he dismissed the Oracle's judgement against him.

Paulina helps ensure that Leontes fully repents for his cruelty to Hermione. Although Leontes is reconciled with Polixenes, Perdita and Hermione at the end of the play, things are obviously still far from the way they would have been had the situation never occurred in the first place. Leontes is still indirectly responsible for the deaths of Mamillius and Antigonus, sixteen years of happiness have been lost and Perdita's parents have missed out on the joy of watching her grow up.

Time and rebirth

Time and rebirth

Shakespeare's main source for *The Winter's Tale* was Robert Greene's novella *Pandosto, The Triumph of Time*. One of the main themes of the play is time as the great healer, or 'the triumph of time' in the cycle of life. Leontes achieves salvation through the passing of time. The concept of time is represented in three ways.

Firstly, to highlight the importance of time, the concept is personified into a character. In his monologue at the beginning of Act 4, Time presents the dual forces of destruction and renewal. Which lines suggest this?

Secondly, there are many references throughout the play to the changes of season. Which season is portrayed in each act? For instance, Act 1 has an autumnal atmosphere. The falling of leaves from the trees, the migration of birds to warmer climates and the preparation of some animals for hibernation all create an atmosphere of loss and separation. Polixenes wants to leave creating a feeling of impending loss (the end of his visit), like the predominating mood of autumn. What other details and events in Act 1 suggest the images and mood of autumn?

Thirdly, the cycle of life is further explored through

many references to the cycle of human life; birth, growth, ageing, decay and death. In Act 1, Polixenes describes his youth with Leontes. In Act 5, Paulina thinks of the ageing, decay and death of her generation when she sees the youthful beauty of Perdita. Keep a note of all references to the passing of time as you read through the play.

Time's healing agent is nature's ability for renewal and rebirth. The theme of rebirth is introduced in Act 4, with the change of focus of the play to Perdita in the natural splendour of rural Bohemia. Her philosophical exchange with Polixenes at the sheep-shearing feast is loaded with images of fertility and growth. Perdita herself represents creation and renewal – her mother's spirit and beauty are renewed in her. Moreover, she is the lost heir of Sicilia and will cure the court's sixteen years of sterility. The idea of rebirth reaches its climax in the final scene of the play, when Hermione is, metaphorically, brought back to life.

Forgiveness

Forgiveness

Forgiveness is the pardoning of blame. The ultimate aim of repentance is forgiveness. This theme is developed in the second half of the play, when Leontes repents, to achieve forgiveness for his original sin. He first asks for forgiveness from Apollo for denying the Oracle's judgement. We hear in Act 4 that Leontes has reconciled himself to Polixenes politically, but not personally. It is not until Act 5 that Leontes is forgiven in succession by the heavens, his lords, Polixenes, Camillo, Perdita, Paulina and finally by Hermione.

You may think that Leontes gets off lightly, having his family restored to him after all the suffering, destruction and death he caused. It is important to remember that humans are mortal, flawed and prone to folly. Continued existence is the victory of life over death, good over evil. Leontes is forgiven because he acknowledges his sins. He takes responsibility for his destruction and accepts that his soul is stained with the blood of his family. He accepts Paulina's criticism and blame, refuses the temptation of remarriage and performs an act of selfless generosity in helping Florizel and Perdita. He has learned through his own suffering and becomes a more virtuous person. He earns his salvation through humility, patience and tolerance.

Romance

The Winter's Tale was probably written about 1611. It is considered one of Shakespeare's last plays and is associated with a group of his later works referred to as 'the romances'. The others romances are *Cymbeline*, *Pericles* and *The Tempest*. The plays share many similar features, for example, having a child of noble birth brought up in a pastoral or rustic setting close to nature and away from courtly life. The pastoral atmosphere of these plays is further reinforced through allusions to Greek and Roman gods. Those who feature in *The Winter's Tale* are Apollo, Proserpina, Neptune and Flora.

Romance as a Shakespearean genre is characterised by a catastrophic, stormy, violent and passionate atmosphere, coupled with a philosophical outlook. All of the plays in this group have these qualities. How are these romantic qualities brought out in the play?

Some critics have said that *The Winter's Tale* presents character types rather than individual portraits. Certainly Florizel is not developed beyond representing young, romantic love and Clown, Shepherd and Autolycus are no more than familiar village types. Leontes' jealousy erupts with no warning preparation or basis, unlike Othello's well-documented jealous arousal by Iago in *Othello*. Shakespeare's examination of jealousy in this play focuses on its destructive consequences, and the relationship between sin and salvation in the cycle of life. The ideas in *The Winter's Tale* are focused beyond the characters, giving the play a timeless quality. How does the word 'tale' in the title of the play convey a timeless dimension?

Structure, balance and context in *The Winter's Tale*

Most of Shakespeare's plays have at least one or two sub-plots running simultaneously alongside the main plot. This is not the case in *The Winter's Tale*. Instead, the play derives its structure from having two main plots, which are distinct from one another in terms of time, but are brought together at the end where each plot is shown to be connected with, and resolved by, the other. The play takes place in three parts. The first part deals with the increasing destruction caused by Leontes' jealousy in Sicilia. The second part of the play concentrates on the natural creative forces in the innocent country life of Bohemia. The final third of the play is the synthesis of the two plots in Sicilia, resulting in the resolution of each.

The sense of balance in the play is achieved in five ways. Firstly, there is a sense of balance in the structure of the play, not from the location, but from the time dimension. Acts 1 to 3 take place 16 years before Acts 4 and 5.

Secondly, there is balance in terms of the atmosphere. The first half of the play is a tragedy caused by Leontes' jealousy and resulting in the apparent death of Hermione and the actual deaths of Mamillius and Antigonus. This atmosphere of tragedy is symbolically washed away by the storm of Act 3, scene 3. This scene marks the transition from destruction to creation, and is simply summed up by Shepherd in the line 'thou met'st with things dying, I with things new born'. The tragic atmosphere is replaced in Act 4 with one of creativity, innocence and harmony with nature. The country setting of Bohemia is presented as an earthly paradise following the hell on earth of Sicilia.

Thirdly, there is balance in the action of the play. Antigonus' death marks the last destructive consequence of Leontes' jealousy. It is immediately followed by Shepherd's discovery of the baby Perdita. Her 'new life' is possible as a result of Antigonus' death.

Fourthly, there is balance within the characters. Florizel and Perdita replace Leontes and Hermione as the main love relationship. Note that Florizel and Perdita are each mentioned in the first half of the play, to prepare us for their eventual appearance and significance.

Finally, a sense of balance is achieved through the idea of contrast presented in the play. Contrast exists in the setting, characters and themes of the play. The court life of Sicilia is contrasted by the nature, harmony and innocence of Bohemia. How do Perdita and Florizel contrast with Hermione and Leontes? Death is replaced with birth. Destruction is redeemed by creation. The balance of opposites is clear.

■ Text commentary

Act 1, scene 1

Polixenes, king of Bohemia, has been enjoying a long stay at the court of his childhood friend Leontes, king of Sicilia. As the play opens, Camillo, a Sicilian lord, and Archidamus, a Bohemian lord, discuss the visit and how much everyone at the two courts has enjoyed it. Archidamus remarks on the promise shown by Prince Mamillius, son of Leontes. Camillo comments on the joy Mamillius brings to the people of Sicilia.

'You shall see, as I have said, great difference betwixt our Bohemia and your Sicilia.'

The play opens with Archidamus' praise of the hospitality he has been shown during his visit to Sicilia. If Camillo visits Bohemia, Archidamus suggests, the hospitality there will surely be inferior. Ironically, Camillo is soon to be leaving for Bohemia and will spend the next sixteen years of his life there. These lines foreshadow Camillo's move to Bohemia.

Camillo

Leontes, the king of Sicilia, is described as a gracious host. What expectations do you have of Leontes from his description in this opening scene?

'Sicilia cannot show himself overkind to Bohemia. They were trained together in their childhoods...'

Often in Shakespeare's plays, kings are referred to by the name of their kingdom. Here, 'Bohemia' refers to Polixenes, king of Bohemia and 'Sicilia' to Leontes, king of Sicilia. In *The Winter's Tale* Bohemia and Sicilia are fictional kingdoms in Europe. They are not the actual countries of Bohemia and Sicily.

Leontes

The two kings were raised together, but royal duties necessitated their separation. Their close bond is emphasised by the imagery of roots and branches.

The main purpose of this opening scene is to provide background information on the two kings. What do we learn of their relationship? Note that Camillo and Archidamus are speaking in prose, not verse. Prose was often used to convey narrative information.

Polixenes

'I think there is not in the world either malice or matter to alter it.'

This opening scene is dominated by the details of Leontes' hospitality and the friendship between the two kings. This line takes on an ironical meaning in the next scene, when a conflict arises which challenges the bond between Leontes and Polixenes.

Act 1, scene 2

Polixenes has been in Sicilia for nine months. He is worried about the state of affairs in his own kingdom during his absence and announces that he must return home. Leontes will not hear of Polixenes' departure, however, and insists that he stay another week. When he cannot convince his friend, Leontes asks his wife, Hermione, to persuade Polixenes to stay. She tells Polixenes that he has no choice in departing, only in deciding whether to stay as her prisoner or her guest. He agrees to stay as her guest. Hermione asks him to tell her about his boyhood with her husband. Leontes becomes jealous that Hermione succeeded where he could not and suspects that his wife and friend are having an affair. Soon, his jealousy gives way to an impassioned rage. He asks Camillo if he knew of the affair, and orders him to poison Polixenes. Camillo believes that Hermione and Polixenes are innocent and he warns the Bohemian king of Leontes' plans. Camillo and Polixenes prepare an immediate secret departure.

'I'll no gainsaying'

Leontes is described at the beginning of the play as a gracious host. Archidamus

Leontes

speaks highly of the hospitality shown to the Bohemian visitors and Polixenes cannot thank Leontes enough for such an enjoyable stay. Leontes' first appearance, however, displays his confident belief in his own power. He insists that Polixenes stays another week and says that he will not accept a refusal.

Leontes is a central character, but he is not introduced until the second scene. Shakespeare often delayed the introduction of main characters until after the opening scene. This strategy creates tension in anticipating their arrival and allows the audience to build expectations of them. Is Leontes as you expected him to be after the opening conversion between Archidamus and Camillo in scene 1? Is the relationship between Leontes and Polixenes in keeping with the description of their relationship in the opening scene?

'There is no tongue that move, none, none i'th'world So soon as yours could win me'

Polixenes' ironic lines form the basis of Leontes' jealousy. It is not Leontes' words which 'move' Polixenes to stay, but those of Hermione.

'...we knew not the doctrine of ill-doing, nor dreamed that any did'

Polixenes describes his youth with Leontes, when they were innocent, carefree

and knew nothing of the suffering that sin brings. He then proceeds to joke about sin with Hermione. Soon after this light exchange Leontes suffers a destructive bout of jealousy, with far-reaching consequences. Leontes ends his friendship with Polixenes; Hermione is humiliated, imprisoned and later

Jealousy and sin   presumed dead of a broken heart; Leontes disowns his own infant daughter and then suffers terrible sadness when he has no family or friends left.

Some critics have argued that Leontes' jealous turn is not convincing because we have not been sufficiently prepared for his change of behaviour. Shakespeare, however, does in fact prepare us for a challenge to Leontes' and Polixenes' friendship as the plot has so far focused exclusively on how close and deep their relationship is. It seems likely that a conflict is going to occur to upset the relationship, as it seems 'too good to be true' and the drama in the play will surround the resolving of the initial conflict.

'He'll stay, my lord.'

Hermione is triumphant where Leontes failed, despite Polixenes' declaration that no-one's words move him more than Leontes'. Leontes tells Hermione that the last time she spoke so successfully she agreed to marry him. Which of Hermione's words could Leontes misconstrue?

Hermione

'Too hot, too hot!
To mingle friendship far is mingling bloods.'

Hermione uses the word 'friend' in referring to Polixenes. In Shakespeare's time, 'friend' could also mean 'lover'. Leontes misinterprets Hermione's words, causing his fit of jealousy. He is immediately convinced that Hermione only succeeded in persuading Polixenes to stay because they are lovers. He even asks his son, Mamillius, for reassurance that he *is* his son. How does Shakespeare make Leontes' sudden jealous turn convincing?

'They're here with me already; whispering, rounding: "Sicilia is a so-forth"'

A 'cuckold' was a popular term in Shakespeare's time and is used in many of his plays. It means a man who has been made a fool of by his wife's adultery.

In his unreasonable state, Leontes believes that everyone in his court knows of Hermione's adultery with Polixenes.

Leontes   Leontes' paranoia further underlines his lapse of sanity.

'I have trusted thee, Camillo,
With all the nearest things to my heart'

Camillo's good judgement stands him as a highly valued lord in Leontes' court,

Camillo

where he serves as an adviser to the king. Camillo agrees to follow Leontes' order to poison Polixenes, but his typical accurate judgement of character prevails and he remains convinced of Hermione's and Polixenes' innocence. He asks for Leontes' assurance that in disposing of Polixenes, Hermione's reputation will be saved.

Note that in the opening scene, Camillo spoke with Archidamus in prose. In this scene he speaks with Leontes in verse. The opening scene is light-hearted in tone. Shakespeare often presented humour and casual conversation through prose, and more serious romance, argument and emotions through verse. Verse also signified the speech of a noble character. Camillo is a noble character, but would be of a lower status than Leontes, Polixenes and Hermione. In this scene he must speak in verse for two reasons: firstly, he is speaking to a more noble character and secondly, the nature of their serious conversation warrants verse.

'I will seem friendly, as thou hast advised me'

Leontes assures Camillo that he will not hurt Hermione's reputation if Polixenes is murdered. Ironically, when Leontes hears of Camillo's and Polixenes' escape from Sicilia, he is further convinced of Hermione's guilt, which leads to her public humiliation and imprisonment.

'This is strange: methinks
My favour here begins to warp.'

Polixenes has noticed the change in Leontes' behaviour. He also recognises

Polixenes

that Camillo is troubled. He guesses that he may be the cause and persuades Camillo to tell him the truth. Camillo convinces Polixenes that it is better to leave than to confront Leontes. Polixenes had prepared his ships for departure and, ironically, he does leave Sicilia at the end of this scene, though not for his original reasons. He, too, hopes that his departure will save

Hermione's honour. Why does Polixenes not defend himself against Leontes' charges? Will his secret departure not look suspicious?

Self-test Questions Act One

Uncover the plot
Delete two of the three alternatives given, to find the correct plot. Beware possible misconceptions and muddles.

Archidamus/Leontes/Polixenes, king of Bohemia/Greece/Sicilia, has been visiting Camillo/Polixenes/Leontes in Bohemia/Norway/Sicilia for nine months. Archidamus, king/lord/prince of Bohemia/Greece/Sicilia, discusses Camillo's possible visit to Greece/Bohemia/Sicilia in the spring/summer/winter. Archidamus/Camillo/Leontes remarks on the promise shown by Mamillius, son of Camillo/Leontes/Polixenes. Archidamus/Florizel/Polixenes is anxious about the state of his kingdom during his absence and decides to return to Bohemia/go to Delphi/stay longer in Sicilia. Leontes/Polixenes/Hermione cannot convince Paulina/Polixenes/Horatio to stay, but Camillo/Ophelia/Hermione is successful. He/she/they tell(s) Archidamus/Leontes/Perdita that he must arrive/leave/stay either as her friend/guest/lover or jailer/patient/prisoner. Hermione/Leontes/Perdita has a sudden fit of generosity/jealousy/shame, suspecting Polixenes and Hermione are enemies/lovers/related. Juliet/Leontes/Polixenes starts behaving comically/rationally/irrationally and asks Archidamus/Camillo/Mamillius if he knew about the affair between Hermione and Archidamus/Phillipa/Polixenes. Hermione/Leontes/Polixenes orders Archidamus/Camillo/Mamillius to poison/stab/strangle Archidamus/Hermione/Polixenes. Archidamus/Camillo/Mamillius agrees, although he is convinced Hermione and Polixenes are guilty/innocent/silly. Archidamus/Camillo/Mamillius tells Hermione/Leontes/Polixenes of Archidamus'/Leontes'/Polixenes' idea/plan/secret. Archidamus/Camillo/Rosalind and Autolycus/Leontes/Polixenes conspire/plan/plot to leave Bohemia/Greece/Sicilia immediately/next week/the next morning.

Who? What? Why? When? Where? How?
1   How much longer does Leontes want Polixenes to stay?
2   How will Camillo ensure Polixenes' escape?
3   Why does Camillo agree to follow Leontes' order to poison Polixenes?
4   Where are Hermione and Polixenes when Leontes is talking to Camillo?
5   How long has Polixenes been visiting Leontes in Sicilia?
6   What is a cuckold?
7   Why would Archidamus serve Camillo 'sleepy' drinks if he visited Bohemia?
8   Why does Leontes remark on the resemblance between himself and Mamillius?
9   To whose betrayal does Polixenes compare his betrayal by Leontes?
10 What does Leontes tell Hermione to say to Polixenes to make him stay?

Who said that, and to whom?
1   'Our praises are our wages'
2   'I'll put my fortunes to your service'
3   'To give mine enemy a lasting wink'
4   'Yet they say we are almost as like as eggs'
5   'The heavens continue their loves!'
6   '…he's all my exercise, my mirth, my matter'
7   'What we changed was innocence for innocence'
8   'Let me know my trespass by its own visage'
9   'Make me not sighted like a basilisk'
10 'To mingle friendship far is mingling bloods'

Open quotes
Identify the scene; complete the phrase; identify the speaker and the character being spoken to.
1   'We were as twinned lambs…'
2   'Oh then my best blood turn to an infected jelly…'
3   'be cured of this diseased opinion…'
4   'I am angling now…'
5   'they that went on crutches ere he was born…'

6 'To satisfy your Highness...'
7 'You put me off with limber vows...'
8 'I would not be a stander-by to hear my sovereign mistress clouded   so...'
9 'Your changed complexions are to me a mirror...'
10 'How sometimes Nature will betray its folly...'

Act 2, scene 1

The following day, Hermione and her ladies-in-waiting are enjoying lighthearted conversation with Mamillius. Hermione is expecting a second baby. Hermione asks Mamillius to tell them a tale and he proceeds to tell them a sad tale for winter. They are interrupted by Leontes, who has just learned of Polixenes' escape with Camillo. Their secret departure in the night convinces Leontes even more of Hermione's and Polixenes' guilt. He takes Mamillius away from Hermione and accuses Polixenes of being the father of her unborn child. He proceeds to accuse her publicly of being an adulteress and orders her to be imprisoned. Hermione makes a brave plea to the court to believe in her innocence and therefore not to cry for her. After Hermione is led away, Antigonus and Leontes' lords try to persuade Leontes of her innocence and the terrible mistake he is making. Leontes is further convinced of Hermione's guilt and has dispatched two lords, Cleomenes and Dion, to the Oracle of Apollo's temple at Delphos to ask the Oracle whether Hermione is innocent or not. Leontes says he will abide by the Oracle's judgement, although he is convinced of his own suspicions.

'The Queen, your mother, rounds apace'

The first lady-in-waiting makes this reference to Hermione's appearance. It is the first indication in the play that she is expecting a second child. Leontes' imminent cruelty to Hermione is made all the more ruthless as he shows no mercy towards her condition.

'Camillo was his help in this, his pander. There is a plot against my life, my crown'

When Leontes hears that Camillo has betrayed his orders and fled with

Polixenes, he becomes paranoid and fears that Camillo had been working for Polixenes for some time. Obviously Leontes now believes that Camillo knew of the adultery and helped Polixenes pursue his affair with Hermione. The paranoid behaviour of Leontes is in keeping with his irrational behaviour. In the last scene Leontes confided his suspicions to Camillo, who claimed to know nothing of the affair. Leontes now believes that Camillo's behaviour in the previous scene was an act.

'Though he does bear some signs of me, yet you have too much blood in him.'

Leontes is now convinced of Hermione's adultery with Polixenes. As before,

Hermione

he makes snide remarks about Mamillius' parentage. His previous remarks were so cryptic that they went unnoticed by the court, but in this instance he makes his doubts clear and direct to Hermione. She is a gentlewoman of high birth and responds to Leontes' cruel and distasteful remark with typical class, poise and quick wit, retaining her honour as best she can by assuming that he is joking with her. Leontes' treatment of Hermione here prepares us for his accusation that Polixenes is the father of Hermione's unborn child, his subsequent imprisonment of Hermione and rejection of his daughter.

Note that this scene started off in a lighthearted vein with gentle joking between Hermione, her ladies-in-waiting and Mamillius. This provides mild comical relief to the tense and serious end of the previous scene. The arrival of Leontes with the news of the secret departure of Polixenes and Camillo creates tension and abruptly changes the tone of the scene. From this point on the tone is grave and serious.

'There's some ill planet reigns; I must be patient, till the heavens look with an aspect more favourable.'

The Elizabethans were very superstitious people, who believed in astrology

Jealousy and sin

much more seriously than we do now. Their view of the world was not centred on humans, as ours is, but on God and nature. When people suffered, they believed that they had either done something to displease God, or that a negative planetary influence was causing turbulence in their lives. They believed very strongly in fate, and so thought that their fate was out of their own control. Hermione believes that there is nothing she can do about Leontes' treatment of her but wait until conditions in the heavens become more favourable.

It was also believed that discord in heaven and the planets resulted in discord between people on earth. An Elizabethan audience would have believed that Leontes brought on the wrath of nature and of God himself through his sin of jealousy.

'... this action I now go on is for my better grace.'

Hermione knows that she is innocent and that Leontes is committing a grave sin against her in his ill judgement. She tells her ladies-in-waiting not to shed any tears for her until she is found guilty. She believes that her suffering is God's will and that she must accept her plight with fortitude, thus demonstrating true grace before God.

The purpose of the first act of any Shakespearean play is to introduce the main characters and the main plot. One purpose of the second plot is to develop the characters. We learn much more about Hermione's character in this scene. She begins with the quick wit and noble demeanour that we saw in the previous scene. Through atrocity, we learn of her deeper virtues of bravery, courage and humility.

'Though I am satisfied, and need no more than what I know, yet shall the oracle give rest to th' minds of others...'

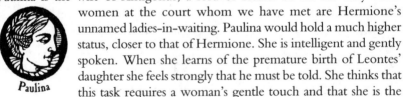

In ancient Greece kings and other persons of high birth would consult the Oracle at Apollo's temple in Delphi with important questions. The Oracle was believed to make infallible predictions and to tell the absolute truth. Leontes' arrogantly believes the Oracle will confirm his suspicions.

Leontes

Antigonus and the other lords try in vain to persuade Leontes to consider the consequences of his behaviour if he is proved wrong. Leontes' irrational thinking causes him to believe too heavily in his own pride. Pride in the face of a higher power, whether it be the Christian God or the gods of antiquity such as Apollo, was a sin called *hubris*. Leontes says that he will accept the Oracle's judgement. Do you believe him?

Notice Shakespeare's use of punctuation to reinforce Leontes' irrational thinking: short sentence fragments separated by dashes, which suggest abrupt thinking and anger. Leontes' reasoning is neither well thought out nor logical.

Act 2, scene 2

Paulina tries to visit Hermione in prison but the jailer has been given orders by Leontes not to allow her any visitors. Paulina asks to at least see one of Hermione's attendants and is permitted to see Emilia, who tells her that Hermione is behaving courageously and that she has given birth, prematurely, to a daughter. Paulina feels that Leontes must be told of the birth and hopes that his harsh treatment of Hermione might be stopped if he saw the innocence of his child.

'If I prove honey-mouthed, let my tongue blister'

Paulina is the wife of Antigonus, a lord of Sicilia. So far the only other women at the court whom we have met are Hermione's unnamed ladies-in-waiting. Paulina would hold a much higher status, closer to that of Hermione. She is intelligent and gently spoken. When she learns of the premature birth of Leontes' daughter she feels strongly that he must be told. She thinks that

Paulina

this task requires a woman's gentle touch and that she is the woman for the job. In accordance with an Elizabethan belief, she swears that if she speaks mere lies, she hopes her tongue will swell with blisters, proving she is sure of herself. Paulina's rational confidence is as strong as Leontes' irrational confidence, and in many ways she proves a character foil to him.

(A character foil is a character, often a minor one, who is in a parallel situation to a major character but who approaches their own situation in a very different way, thus highlighting the opposite qualities in the major character. How does Paulina prove to be a character foil to Leontes?)

'The silence often of pure innocence persuades, when speaking fails'

Paulina hopes that the baby's innocence will move Leontes to return to his senses and undo all the ridiculous harm that he has caused. Tragically, however, her plan backfires. Instead of being moved, Leontes is disgusted, believing the child to be Polixenes' daughter. Ironically, Paulina's plan results in Leontes ordering to have the baby killed, thus extending the destructive power of his jealousy even further.

Jealousy and sin

Act 2, scene 3

Leontes says that he cannot rest until either Polixenes or Hermione has been punished for their adultery. As Polixenes has escaped from Sicilia, Leontes will have to be satisfied with punishing Hermione. Prince Mamillius is ill, and Leontes believes it is due to the shame the child's mother has brought on him. He believes that Polixenes, Camillo and Hermione are laughing at him.

Paulina demands to see Leontes and show him the baby. The servant warns her that Leontes has not slept all night and is in no condition to see anyone. Leontes rejects the infant as Polixenes' bastard child, although Paulina tries to convince Leontes that he is the baby's father by pointing out how much the child resembles him. Leontes orders her to be silent and threatens to have her burned as a witch. Paulina warns him that his tyrannical behaviour will damage his own reputation, and leaves the child with him. Leontes orders Antigonus to set fire to the baby, accusing him of sending Paulina to him with the child. When the other lords defend Antigonus, Leontes calls them all liars. One of the lords convinces Leontes of their loyalty and says that burning the baby is too horrible a death, which will only lead to terrible consequences. Leontes relents and instead orders Antigonus to abandon the child in a deserted land and leave its survival to chance. Antigonus hopes that nature will take pity on the baby. A servant announces that Cleomenes and Dion have returned from visiting the Oracle and are on their way to the court. Leontes orders a public trial for Hermione.

'He straight declined, drooped, took it deeply, Fastened, and fixed the shame on 't in himself'

Mamillius is ill, and Leontes believes that it is due to the shame that Hermione has brought on them. Of course, the young prince's illness is due to worry and strain over his mother's imprisonment. Leontes is so blinded by his own jealousy he cannot see the truth – that it is he who has caused Mamillius' suffering, not Hermione. Jealousy is a terrible emotion, because it hurts and destroys the lives of many innocent people such as Mamillius.

Jealousy and sin

'Commit me for committing honour'

When Paulina brings Leontes his new daughter, he tries to resist seeing her.

He had ordered Antigonus to keep Paulina away from him and Antigonus does warn her, but he knows his wife's strong will. Leontes is surprised that Antigonus does not rule his wife. Paulina replies that Antigonus cannot order her against acting honourably, as Leontes has done to Hermione.

Paulina

There appears to be much more equality in Antigonus' and Paulina's marriage than in that of Leontes and Hermione. Antigonus does not have the dominance over Paulina that Leontes has over Hermione. Paulina further emphasises Leontes' abuse of power in implying sarcastically that he has imprisoned Hermione only to satisfy his own will.

A pun is a play on words. Shakespeare used many puns, usually to create humour. Paulina makes a pun on the word 'commit', using it first to mean being sent to prison. She then uses 'committing' to mean 'performing'.

'...take it hence, and see it instantly consumed with fire.'

Leontes believes that Antigonus arranged for Paulina to show him the baby.

He calls Antigonus a traitor and orders him to burn the baby to death as his punishment and bring back evidence that he has done so. Furthermore, he threatens that if Antigonus does not follow his orders, he will kill him and dash out the child's brains himself. Paulina had said that she would not call Leontes a tyrant, but his behaviour has clearly become tyrannical. This

Leontes

behaviour shows how unhinged his mind has become. He is so consumed by jealousy that he cannot sleep. This further impairs his judgement and feeds his crazy behaviour.

We know that the child is his and that his jealousy has blinded him to the truth. He refers throughout the scene to the child as 'bastard', 'brat' and 'it'. In Shakespeare's day, heretics (people who acted against the Church) and witches were burned to death. In ordering the baby to this terrible fate, Leontes believes the child is evil as a result of being a bastard. This highlights the deep irrationality of his thinking, his abuse of royal power and his potential for cruelty. Ironically, had the innocent child been burned alive, it would have been Leontes committing an act of evil.

'That thou commend it strangely to some place,
Where chance may nurse or end it.'

Antigonus and the other lords plead with Leontes to spare the child from the fire. He finally relents and changes the baby's fate to being abandoned in a strange, deserted country where its survival is left to nature's will. In doing this, Leontes is not committing first degree murder. Abandonment is not as great a sin as murder, thus allowing him to be forgiven at the end of the play.

'Summon a session, that we may arraign our most disloyal lady'

Dion and Cleomenes have returned from Delphos with the Oracle's judgement and are on their way to the court. Leontes orders a public trial for Hermione, convinced that she is guilty and that the Oracle will confirm his suspicions. It never occurs to him that in making the trial public, he could be condemning himself if the Oracle finds Hermione innocent. The trial will

Jealousy and sin complete Hermione's public humiliation and have tragic consequences. Ironically, Leontes says that she will have 'a just and open trial'. Given his behaviour in this scene, do you believe this is possible?

Self-test Questions Act Two

Uncover the plot
Delete two of the three alternatives given, to find the correct plot. Beware possible misconceptions and muddles.
Emilia/Hermione/Paulina and her ladies-in-waiting are being entertained by Antigonus/Leontes/Mamillius. Cecilia/Hermione/Phillipa asks Autolycus/Leontes/Mamillius to tell a tale. He says that a happy/romantic/sad tale is best for spring/summer/winter. They are interrupted by the arrival of Leontes and his lords. He has just learned of the secret departure/meeting/wedding of Polixenes and Camillo. Antigonus/Leontes/Mamillius believes that Camillo's betrayal of his orders proves more strongly that Antigonus/Archidamus/Polixenes is guilty/innocent/indifferent. Leontes mistakenly/privately/publicly humiliates Emilia/Hermione/Paulina. He says she has been dishonest/unfaithful/unkind and orders her to bed/leave/prison. She reacts bravely/calmly/shamefully to her imprisonment/pregnancy/separation. Antigonus/Archidamus/Camillo defends Cecilia's/Hermione's/Paulina's innocence. Antigonus/Archidamus/Florizel says that if Emilia/Hermione/Paulina is guilty of adultery, then he will keep his own daughters/sons/wife attached to him by a leash. To prove that his judgement is right, Antigonus/Leontes/Mamillius has sent two lords to the fortune teller/Oracle/prophet at Bohemia/Delphos/Sicilia.
Emilia/Leontes/Paulina, wife of Antigonus/Archidamus/Camillo, tries to visit Camillo/Hermione/Polixenes. The guard/jailer/soldier has orders not to permit anyone/Paulina/Cecilia to visit the king/prince/queen. She is able to see Emilia, an attendant to the queen. Emilia tells her that the king/prince/queen has given

birth/in/up. Paulina believes that if Rosalind/Leontes/Polixenes saw the innocence of the baby/prince/queen then he would be moved to retract his accusation against Camillo/Hermione/Hamlet and return to his home/senses/wife.

Antigonus/Leontes/Mamillius/cannot sleep. He will find no peace until Antigonus/Hermione/Juliet is punished. Emilia/Hero/Paulina shows him the baby. He calls it a bastard/blessing/princess and orders it to be burned/poisoned/spared. He calls his lords loyal/servants/traitors, but they say that burning the child to death is too cruel/difficult/hot and will have favourable/no/terrible consequences. Leontes instead orders the child to be abandoned/strangled/fed. Dion and Antigonus/Camillo/Cleomenes return from Bohemia/Delphos/Sicilia. Leontes calls for a public celebration/execution/trial for Dion/Hermione/Paulina.

Who? What? Why? When? Where? How?
1   Who does Leontes think are laughing at him?
2   What does Antigonus warn will happen if Leontes' judgement is wrong?
3   How long have Dion and Cleomenes been gone?
4   How does Paulina misjudge the extent of Leontes' jealousy?
5   Where is the Oracle of Apollo?
6   Where is Antigonus to abandon the baby?
7   How does Paulina persuade the jailer to let her take the baby out of prison?
8   Why has Hermione given birth prematurely?
9   Why can't Leontes sleep?
10 Why does Hermione tell her ladies-in-waiting not to cry for her?

Who said that, and to whom?
1   'A nest of traitors'
2   'Every dram of woman's flesh is false, if she be'
3   'I come to bring him sleep'
4   'Either thou art most ignorant by age, or thou wert born a fool'
5   'I learned it out of women's faces'
6   'While she lives, my heart will be a burden to me'
7   'No court in Europe is too good for thee'
8   'My poor prisoner, I am as innocent as you'
9   '…and no less honest than you are mad'
10 I have drunk, and seen the spider'

Open Quotes
Identify the scene; complete the phrase; identify the speaker and the character being spoken to.
1   'It is an heretic that makes the fire…'
2   'The centre is not big enough to bear a schoolboy's top.'
3   '…but she, I can hook to me…'
4   'Be certain what you do, sir…'
5   'A sad tale's best for winter…'
6   'I'll pawn the little blood which I have left…'
7   'if wit flow from't as boldness from my bosom…'
8   'Here's such ado to make no stain a stain…'
9   'Come on, poor babe, some powerful spirit instruct the kites and ravens…'
10 'I am not prone to weeping, as our sex commonly are…'

Act 3, scene 1

Cleomenes and Dion are travelling along a high road on their way from the port to Leontes' court in Sicilia. They discuss their trip to Delphos. The climate was pleasing and the Oracle itself was very impressive. They believe Hermione is innocent and are hopeful that the Oracle will provide the proof to end this terrible ordeal. They hurry back, as they know that the court awaits the Oracle's judgement.

'these proclamations, so forcing faults upon Hermione, I little like.'

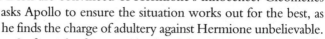

Cleomenes and Dion are convinced of Hermione's innocence. Cleomenes asks Apollo to ensure the situation works out for the best, as he finds the charge of adultery against Hermione unbelievable.

So far each of Leontes' lords, while still loyal to him in their duties, believes Hermione is innocent. Leontes is the only person in Sicilia to think ill of her — further evidence of his impaired judgement. Leontes has sworn to adhere to the Oracle's judgement. If it finds Hermione innocent, how do you think he will react? Suspense is created as we anticipate the Oracle's answer.

Leontes

Act 3, scene 2

Leontes opens the trial in a court of justice. Hermione is led in and is charged with high treason in committing adultery with Polixenes, conspiring with Camillo to kill Leontes and helping Polixenes and Camillo to escape. Pleading not guilty to the charges, Hermione is defending her life, but more importantly, her honour. Hermione speaks well, but her husband is not moved. He announces that he has cast out the new baby. Hermione calls for the Oracle to be read. Cleomenes and Dion are brought into the court with the sealed judgement. The Oracle deems Hermione, Polixenes and Camillo innocent of all charges. It also confirms that Leontes is the father of Hermione's baby and that he will be without an heir unless the baby is found. Finally, the Oracle pronounces Leontes a jealous tyrant.

Leontes dismisses the Oracle as false. A servant brings news of Mamillius' death. Upon hearing this news, Leontes realises it is he who has sinned. Hermione faints and is removed from the courtroom. Leontes begs Apollo for forgiveness and publicly redeems the good names of Polixenes and Camillo. He realises why Camillo really left Sicilia. Paulina scolds him for being a tyrant and announces that the queen has died. Leontes agrees with Paulina's harsh judgement. He vows to visit the graves of Hermione and Mamillius every day and says he will dedicate the rest of his life to mourning their deaths.

'For life, I prize it
As I weigh grief, which I would spare; for honour,
'Tis a derivative from me to mine,'

This is the first time we have seen Hermione since she was sent to prison and gave birth. She pleads 'not guilty' to the charges against her, speaking with fortitude and composure in her defence. She says that her life means as much to her as grief which she would gladly end. She must defend her honour,

Hermione

because her reputation will affect her children. Hermione's words are tragically prophetic, because her son Mamillius dies immediately after Leontes has rejected the Oracle's clearing of Hermione's good name. The servant reports that he died over concern for his mother's well-being.

Hermione reiterates this sentiment in her closing remarks on the stand. Compare her behaviour and speech in the court of justice with that of Leontes. Hermione has spoken with dignity and reason throughout the play. In contrast, Leontes has spoken with increasingly impassioned rage.

'The Prince, your son, with mere conceit and fear Of the Queen's speed, is gone.'

Jealousy and sin

Prince Mamillius dies immediately after Leontes has rejected the judgement of the Oracle. He had been sick ever since his mother was imprisoned. The servant reports that he died of fear over Hermione's fate. His innocent death demonstrates the tragic destructive power of jealousy. Leontes has spared no concern for how his treatment of Hermione would affect his son. Mamillius' illness and death are evidence of the disorder that the kingdom has been in since the onset of Leontes' jealousy.

In Shakespeare's romances and comedies, the circumstances of the main characters become increasingly worse and more complicated throughout the first three acts. They reach their climax of disorder in Act 3. Mamillius' death represents the climax of Leontes' evil. Conditions will start to improve and be resolved in Act 4.

'Apollo, pardon my great profaneness 'gainst thine oracle.'

It takes Mamillius' death to bring Leontes to his senses. He realises that it is he who has sinned, especially in rejecting the truth of the Oracle. He asks for Apollo's forgiveness, promising to reconcile with Polixenes, treat Hermione well and recall Camillo back to Sicilia. He goes on in this speech to

Forgiveness

acknowledge the great honour Camillo did in ignoring his orders to kill Polixenes. Had Camillo carried out these orders, Leontes would have the murder of an innocent man on his hands, in addition to the cruelty he has done to Hermione, Mamillius and his daughter. He understands that Camillo had to leave Sicilia for his own safety and that he gave up a great deal in order spare Polixenes' life and Leontes' honour.

Leontes believes that his son's death could be his punishment from Apollo for rejecting his judgement. He has already cast his only other child out of his kingdom. He does not want to lose anyone else.

It is interesting to note that Leontes does not send another boat out to catch up with Antigonus and stop him from abandoning the baby. Nor does he go to Hermione to comfort her or even pray for her after she has fainted and ask for her forgiveness. His transition is not yet complete, as his first thought is still for himself.

The sweet'st, dear'st creature's dead; and vengeance for 't Not dropped down yet.'

Paulina is quick to point out the damage that Leontes' jealousy has caused.

She tells him that he has lost his daughter, son and wife. This is the first time that she says that Hermione is dead, implying that Leontes is responsible, and warns that divine retribution for his sins has not yet been handed out.

Paulina

Paulina speaks her mind in her harsh criticism of Leontes. She swore in the previous scene that she would not call him a tyrant, but she feels that he went too far in rejecting the Oracle's judgement and calls him a tyrant now. She is a well respected woman in Sicilia and no doubt her honest opinion of Leontes contributes to his return to reason.

'and still winter in storm perpetual, Could not move the gods to look that way thou wert.'

The imagery of the storm which Paulina uses to warn Leontes of the repercussions of his guilt foreshadows the real storm in the following scene.

'Thou canst not speak too much, I have deserved All tongues to talk their bitt'rest.'

Leontes agrees with Paulina's harsh assessment of his behaviour. In these lines we witness the start of a change in his character from a jealous tyrant to a rational and humble man. His regaining of his reason happens almost as suddenly as his jealousy came on. In Act 1, scene 2 he was sure that everyone was secretly laughing at him. Now he accepts that people should speak badly of him.

Leontes

'Alas, I have showed too much The rashness of a woman; he is touched to th' noble heart.'

Paulina is the first person to accept that Leontes has changed for the better.

She forgives him when she sees that he is acting nobly and regretting his sins. She apologises for being so rash with him and says she will now become his faithful servant.

Forgiveness

Paulina shares many character traits with Leontes. She displayed impassioned behaviour at the injustice of Hermione's death, and returns to her rational self more quickly than Leontes. She represents realistic human behaviour as a mix of the emotional and rational. Leontes' jealous turn represents the damage caused by passions being pushed to the extreme.

**'Thou didst speak but well,
When most the truth which I receive much better
Than to be pitied of thee.'**

Leontes acknowledges that Paulina spoke the truth to him. He would rather that she was honest with him than pity him. Leontes' change of heart is now complete. He says he will now dedicate the rest of his life to mourning the deaths of Hermione and Mamillius.

Repentance

Act 3, scene 3

A storm is threatening when Antigonus arrives on the shores of Bohemia. He has had a disturbing dream about Hermione, in which she warned him that he will never see Paulina again because of his involvement in abandoning the baby. Worried by the dream, Antigonus believes Hermione's death proves that she was guilty of adultery with Polixenes. He leaves the baby with identity documents and gold nearby. On his way back to the ship, he is mauled to death and half eaten by a bear. A shepherd searching for his lost sheep finds the baby and remarks on her beauty. His son, Clown, joins him after seeing Leontes' ship wrecked in the storm and Antigonus being killed by the bear. They believe the gold left with Perdita, the baby, is fairy gold and agree to keep it a secret. They will take the child home. Clown will bury Antigonus' remains.

'thy mother appeared to me last night'

Antigonus believes that Hermione must be dead when she appears to him in a dream. How does his seeing 'dead' Hermione in his dream help to convince us that she is dead?

'For this ungentle business
Put on thee by my lord, thou ne'er shalt see
Thy wife Paulina more.'

This is the warning that Antigonus receives in the dream from Hermione. In

the dream she appeared very real. He believes the dream, but still goes ahead with abandoning the baby because he believes that Hermione's death is evidence of her guilt in committing adultery with Polixenes, thereby making Perdita a bastard. In Shakespeare's day illegitimate children were labelled 'bastards'

Jealousy and sin and treated cruelly, hence the insult of calling someone a bastard. The bastards of noblemen were often never officially, if personally, acknowledged. If Perdita really was illegitimate, Elizabethan audiences would have understood and accepted Leontes' desire to 'get rid of it'.

Antigonus had already embarked on his voyage when the court case was heard. He did not hear Apollo's judgement, or witness Hermione's death of a broken heart at the news of Mamillius' death. Antigonus only knows that Hermione is dead from his dream. He misunderstands her death and falsely believes Perdita to be a bastard, thereby making his act of abandonment an act of evil. There are many indications in this scene that what Antigonus is doing is wrong. At the start of the scene, the mariner comments that the brewing storm shows God's disapproval of what they are doing. Antigonus admits that his heart bleeds for his involvement in abandoning Perdita and right before his death, he comments on the violence of the storm: 'I never saw the heavens so dim by day.' His violent death appears to be his punishment, and Hermione's prediction has come true as he will never see Paulina again. Leontes' jealousy has caused the deaths of Antigonus and all the crew on the ship which was wrecked in the storm. All the deaths incurred as a result of Leontes' jealousy are symbolic of the destructive power of jealousy.

'A pretty one, a very pretty one'

These are the shepherd's first words when he discovers Perdita. Her beauty

Perdita

is already evident, as it is the first thing he notices. He recognises that she is wearing the christening gown of a nobleman and concludes that her abandonment means that she is illegitimate. When he discovers the gold he believes that she was stolen by fairies and that the gold is a gift from them. People of those times believed that supernatural gifts must be kept secret or they might by taken away. Right from her arrival in Bohemia, Perdita is regarded as very special.

No doubt Shepherd and Clown are illiterate, so that they are unable to read the documents found with the infant. Why is it important that they do not know Perdita's true identity?

'...thou met'st things dying, I with things new born.'

This scene marks the transition from the setting of Sicilia to Bohemia. All the

Time and rebirth

destruction and death associated with Sicilia have now been left behind. In Bohemia, Leontes' sin will start to be resolved, and the theme of rebirth introduced. Although simple, the shepherd has already noticed the powers of rebirth operating. This, he says, is symbolised by Clown's witnessing death in the form of Antigonus' murder and the shipwreck whilst he discovered new life, the baby Perdita.

Shepherd's words are philosophical but are said in prose. Compare them with Antigonus' verse at the start of the scene. The transition in setting from Sicilia to Bohemia is further reinforced by the switch in the middle of the scene from verse to prose.

Self-test Questions Act Three

Uncover the plot
Delete two of the three alternatives given, to find the correct plot. Beware possible misconceptions and muddles.

Antigonus/Cleomenes/Dion remarks on the beauty of the island of Delphos, while Antony/Cleomenes/Dion describes the pomp and ceremony of the Oracle. Antigonus/Cleomenes/Caesar asks Apollo/God/Jove to end Emilia's/Hermione's/Paulina's suffering.

Cleomenes/Brutus/Leontes opens the proceedings at the court of justice. Emilia/Hermione/Paulina is charged with high treason in committing adultery with Camillo/Leontes/Polixenes, conspiring with Antigonus/Camillo/Polixenes to kill Leontes and helping Camillo and Polixenes to escape. Hermione pleads not guilty and says that she is fighting for her dignity/honour/life. Leontes tells her that he has cast out Antigonus/Mamillius/the baby. Hermione/Leontes/Paulina calls for the charge/Oracle/punishment to be read out. The Oracle finds Hermione guilty/chaste/truthful, Polixenes blameless/harmless/a cheat and Camillo barbaric/silly/a true subject. Leontes is found to be a jealous friend/king/tyrant who accepts/praises/rejects the Oracle's judgement. A servant announces that Antigonus/Hermione/Mamillius has died, and Hermione/Leontes/Paulina faints. Emilia/Hermione/Paulina scolds Leontes harshly for his tyrannical behaviour, but he accepts/dismisses/rejects her judgement. His conceit/jealousy/nobility returns and he says that he will visit Hermione's and Mamillius' graves every day/every week/every year.

Antigonus/Camillo/Leontes arrives on the coast of Bohemia/Delphos/Sicilia, where a fire/storm/volcano is threatening. He has had a terrible dream. Emilia/Hermione/Perdita warned him that if he carries out Camillo's/Leontes'/Polixenes' orders then he will never see Leontes/Paulina/Sicilia again. He follows the orders because he believes that Florizel/Mamillius/Perdita is illegitimate. On his way back to the carriage/horse/ship he is pursued and half eaten by a bear/lion/tiger. Shepherd finds Perdita whilst his son Clown/Florizel/Mamillius witnesses the shipwreck and Antigonus'/Hermione's/Leontes' death. They believe the baby was left as a curse/gift/warning by fairies/gnomes/witches, so that they must keep it a secret. Shepherd takes the baby home/to Polixenes/to the ship.

Who? What? Why? When? Where? How?
1 How many people has Leontes lost through his jealousy?
2 What has Mamillius died from?
3 How are Dion and Cleomenes travelling to the court?
4 How does Leontes say he will spend the rest of his days?
5 Where has Perdita been abandoned?
6 Who is Hermione's father?
7 What did the Oracle's voice sound like?
8 From what sin did Camillo save Leontes?
9 Why must Perdita's true origins and the gold be kept secret?
10 When will Leontes get an heir?

Who said that, and to whom?
1 'the heavens with that we have in hand are angry and frown upon 's.'
2 'You speak a language that I understand not.'
3 'Of all that hear me, and my near'st of kin cry fie upon my grave!'
4 '...and tears shed there shall be my recreation.'
5 '...this place is famous for the creatures of prey that keep upon 't.'

6 'Tis rigor, and not law.'
7 'How ceremonious, solemn, and unearthly it was I' th' off'ring!'
8 'What studied torments, tyrant, hast for me?'
9 '...it was told me I should be rich by the fairies.'
10 'I have too much believed my own suspicion.'

Open quotes
Identify the scene; complete the phrase; identify the speaker and the character being spoken to.
1 '...there these, which may, if Fortune please, both breed thee, pretty...'
2 '...the King shall live without as heir...'
3 'Innocence shall make False Accusation blush...'
4 'Thou canst not speak too much...'
5 ''Tis a lucky day, boy...'
6 'The sessions shall proceed...'
7 'The climate's delicate, the air most sweet, fertile the isle...'
8 'and still winter in storm perpetual...'
9 'Weep I cannot, but my heart bleeds...'
10 'And how his piety...'

Act 4, scene 1

Time, personified with wings and an hourglass in one hand, announces that sixteen years have passed. Leontes has grieved all these years, Polixenes' son Florizel has grown up and Perdita has grown into a beautiful young woman. The action of the play now concentrates on Perdita.

'A shepherd's daughter,
And what to her adheres, which follows after,
Is th' argument of Time.'

The action of the play now shifts from Leontes and his court at Sicilia to Perdita and the land of Bohemia. The play is balanced in that the first three acts concern Leontes and the damage that his jealousy causes.

Acts 4 and 5 are equal in length to the first three scenes and will concern the resolving of damage done by Leontes. Sixteen years have passed and the shift in focus to the younger generation of Bohemia and Sicilia represents the cycle of

Time and rebirth rebirth. The love affair between Perdita and Florizel represents the resolving of the friendship between the two countries. Note too that the setting of Act 4 is the country, and pay attention to all the references to spring and new life.

Shakespeare had to use the character of time personified to represent the passing of time. This character is in the tradition of the Greek chorus of the classic plays of Greek antiquity, when the chorus would come on stage and tell the audience what was going to happen in each scene. This helped reinforce the plot and themes of the play for the audience.

In Shakespeare's comedies and romances, a turning point for the better in the plot would occur in the third act. This occurs in *The Winter's Tale* in the middle of Act 3, scene 3 when we meet Shepherd and Clown. The scene is set in Bohemia, but the first half of the scene still concerns the court of Leontes, as represented through Antigonus. After his death, the last death in the play, the focus shifts from Leontes and death to Perdita and rebirth. From this point on all the conflicts in the plot will be resolved.

Act 4, scene 2

Camillo has served Polixenes well, but now after sixteen years desires to return to Sicilia. Polixenes tries to convince him to stay in Bohemia and help him discover why his son Florizel is ignoring his courtly duties in favour of spending time at the home of an uncharacteristically wealthy shepherd. Both men have heard that the shepherd has a beautiful daughter. He proposes that they disguise themselves and pay a visit to the shepherd. Camillo agrees to lay his thoughts of Sicilia to one side and help Polixenes.

'the report of her is extended more than can be thought to begin from such a cottage.'

Camillo has heard of the reputed beauty of Perdita, daughter of Shepherd. Her beauty is so rare that it is hard to believe that she is the daughter of such a simple and common man. In the previous scene, Shepherd first noticed her beauty as a baby and now, sixteen years on, she has a reputation in Bohemia for her exquisite beauty and gentleness. Already, there are indications that Perdita is not who she seems to be. Such remarks prepare the other characters for the revelation of her true identity.

Perdita

'I fear, the angle that plucks our son thither.'

Florizel is now grown into a young man. Polixenes is afraid that Prince Florizel has fallen in love with the peasant daughter of the shepherd. Although she is beautiful, her low birth does not make her a suitable candidate for a prince's bride. Florizel is spending so much time with her that Polixenes is concerned that his feelings are more than a passing fancy. These details prepare us for the depth of love between the two young people. They will leave Bohemia in order to remain together.

Florizel

The audience knows that Perdita's true identity makes her a suitable bride for Florizel. This is called dramatic irony, when the audience knows something which the characters on stage do not. We know that it is possible for Perdita's true identity to be revealed, thereby making possible the romance between her and Florizel. After the tragedies of the first three acts, we anticipate a happy ending for Perdita and Florizel.

No doubt Florizel has noticed Perdita's natural refinement and is attracted to more than her beauty alone. In Shakespeare's day, the class system was much more rigid than it is today. People rarely married someone from a different class. Beauty alone would not have been enough to hold a nobleman's interest without other indications of noble birth.

'Prithee be my present partner in this business'

Polixenes has had Florizel followed by a courtier to report on his business at

the shepherd's house. Polixenes fears that his son is attracted to the peasant girl and now feels that it is time to intervene. He asks Camillo to help him spy on Florizel and talk to the old shepherd. It is immoral of Polixenes to want to spy on his son. His request to Camillo to join him faintly echoes Leontes' order to Camillo in Act 1 to murder Polixenes. Presumably

Polixenes is unable to confront Florizel directly about his interests away from the court because he is so seldom at the court. What have we learned about Polixenes' character in this scene? Why is he worried about Florizel?

Note that throughout this scene Polixenes and Camillo have spoken to one another in prose and not the usual verse which distinguishes noble characters. Think about the reason why prose is being used instead of verse.

'and lay aside the thoughts of Sicilia.'

Ironically, it is through accompanying Polixenes in his plan to discover Florizel's business at the cottage of the old shepherd, that Camillo has the opportunity to return to Sicilia. Why has Shakespeare reminded us of Sicilia at this point in the play?

Camillo

Act 4, scene 3

Autolycus, a thief, is walking near Shepherd's cottage singing a song about his dishonest ways. He meets Clown, who is on his way to do some shopping for the sheep-shearing feast. Autolycus deceives Clown by saying that he has been robbed by a thief named Autolycus. He picks Clown's pocket and after being told of the sheep-shearing contest, decides to attend it to steal from other shepherds.

Act 4, scene 4

It is the sheep-shearing contest. Perdita, dressed as the Queen of the Feast, and Florizel, dressed as a shepherd, declare their love for one another. Perdita is worried about Polixenes discovering their romance. Their private conversation is interrupted by the guests and Shepherd, who asks Perdita to welcome them. Among the guests are Polixenes and Camillo in disguise. Polixenes speaks to Perdita about flowers, but is really giving her a warning about the problems of marrying out of one's class. Polixenes and Camillo are both struck by Perdita's beauty and acknowledge that she has a nobility uncharacteristic of simple shepherdesses. A dance is performed by the shepherds and shepherdesses, in which Perdita and Florizel take part. During the dance, Polixenes asks Shepherd about the young man dancing with his daughter and Shepherd replies that the young man loves her.

A servant announces the arrival of a pedlar, Autolycus. He sells his wares to the willing shepherds, but his business is interrupted by the performance of a masque (a dramatic entertainment) called 'The Twelve Satyrs'. Florizel tells Shepherd and the disguised Polixenes of his wish to be engaged to Perdita. Polixenes asks him if he is going to tell his father. Although he does not acknowledge that his father is the king, Florizel replies that he has good reasons not to tell him. At this, Polixenes reveals his identity and forbids Florizel from ever seeing Perdita again. Before he departs, he threatens Perdita with death if she should ever try to come near Florizel again. Perdita orders Florizel to go, but he declares that he would rather have her love than be the king's heir. Camillo suggests that they go to Sicilia to be received by Leontes.

Autolycus returns, bragging to himself of his sales that day. Camillo offers Autolycus money to exchange clothes with Florizel so that he will not be recognised on his way to Sicilia. Camillo confesses to himself that his real intention in helping the young couple escape to Sicilia is to have Polixenes follow them, thereby creating the opportunity for Camillo to return to his homeland. Florizel, Perdita and Camillo depart, leaving Autolycus on his own. He has overheard enough of their conversation to guess their plan. Meanwhile Shepherd and Clown, frightened by Polixenes' threats, are on their way to his court with documents proving Perdita's real identity. They meet Autolycus, dressed in Florizel's clothing, and he fools them into believing that he is from the court. He asks them their business and when told they are on their way to see the king he says that he can arrange a meeting – for a fee. Realising that he could extort money out of Florizel for keeping Shepherd, Clown and their documents away from Polixenes, Autolycus deceives them about the king's whereabouts, misdirecting them to the ship setting sail for Sicilia.

'For you there's rosemary and rue; these keep seeming and savour all the winter long.'

Perdita is dressed as the queen of the sheep-shearing competition. Shepherd has asked her to welcome the guests as his wife used to. She welcomes the disguised Polixenes and Camillo with flowers. It is the end of summer and she gives the men rue and rosemary, whose colour and scent will last throughout the winter.

Forgiveness

The choice of flowers is meaningful. Rue was given for grace and repentance. Rosemary was given for remembrance, because the fragrance lasted a long time. The qualities of the flowers prepare us for the reconciliation of Polixenes and Camillo with Leontes. The reason for their original departure from Sicilia will be remembered, but the men will forgive one another and be reconciled. It is metaphorically significant that Perdita gives them the flowers, as she is the reason that they travel to Sicilia. The eventual marriage between Perdita and Florizel will reinforce the reconciliation between the two countries.

Perdita mentions winter, which reminds us of the change of seasons. This is symbolic of the passing of time and the many changes of seasons which have taken place between her birth and the present time.

'Of trembling winter, the fairest flow'rs o' th' season
Are our carnations, and streaked gillyvors,
Which some call nature's bastards...'

Polixenes, in disguise, is meeting Perdita for the first time. He immediately

Perdita

comments on her beauty and talks to her about flowers. The conversation is only superficially about flowers, however – underlying it is a philosophical discussion about nature. The flowers Perdita mentions are streaked with colour and therefore have associations with loose, 'painted' women. By saying that there is no place in their garden for such flowers, she is asserting her own gentleness and grace.

The reader is also meeting Perdita, as a young woman, for the first time. She has grown up in the country unaware of her true identity. The country is associated with nature and pastoral harmony – pastoral settings often symbolise an earthly garden of Eden. In this scene, Perdita is frequently associated with flowers, which, along with her beauty and her rustic upbringing, present her as an almost divine creation. Her status of queen of the feast foreshadows her future title of Queen of Bohemia.

Polixenes goes on to speak of mixing wild flowers with cultivated varieties, saying that these mixings produce a baser stock than the cultivated parent. He is obviously referring to his concerns about Florizel's high birth and background being genetically mixed with Perdita's common upbringing. She responds intelligently to his ideas, thereby asserting her 'natural' dignity.

'I will devise a death as cruel for thee
As thou art tender to 't.'

Polixenes is happy for Florizel to have an affair with a beautiful shepherdess,

Polixenes

but marriage would be out of the question. His sudden rage at the idea of his son marrying Perdita echoes Leontes' jealous rage in Act 1, scene 2. He threatens Perdita with a cruel death, just as Leontes treated Hermione cruelly. A Shakespearean audience would have expected Polixenes to react with such vehemence, as it was unthinkable for royalty to marry down into the ranks of the peasantry. The two kings share many similarities. They both doted on their infant sons and they both misuse their regal power in order to control others. Like Leontes, Polixenes' temper will cost him his son, as Florizel chooses to forsake his father in order to marry Perdita. At the end of the play, both men will be reconciled with the children they lost through fits of rage.

'Being now awake, I'll queen it no inch farther, But milk my ewes, and weep.'

Perdita

When Polixenes forbids Florizel from marrying Perdita and threatens her with death, she responds by honouring Polixenes' judgement (although she does not agree with it) and asking Florizel to leave. Which lines shows that Perdita is not afraid of Polixenes? Her personal dignity prevents her from entertaining any ideas above her station. She has always anticipated Polixenes' discovering their romance, and now that he has, she will unselfishly give up her dream of marrying her prince. Her brave behaviour in the face of adversity recalls Hermione's courage. Perdita has a natural sense of humility which keeps her from a false sense of importance, despite the numerous compliments she receives about her beauty and demeanour.

'From my succession wipe me, father, I Am heir to my affection.'

Florizel

Florizel demonstrates the depth of his feeling for Perdita in declaring that he would rather be with her than become the next king of Bohemia. Unlike his father, he is not interested in the trappings of power and wealth: he values love more highly. Critics could argue that Florizel is letting his emotions rule his reason. In this respect, he would be like Leontes. His decision is logical, however, because he says a few lines later that it would be madness if he did not follow his 'fancy' (his heart).

This is also the first scene in which we meet Florizel. Although not perhaps as impressive as Perdita, he reveals himself to be an honest, honourable and romantic young man.

'embrace but my direction, if your more ponderous and settled project May suffer alteration.'

Camillo

In desperation, Florizel appeals to Camillo to help him escape from his father and marry his beloved Perdita. Camillo is respected by all as a man of good judgement and honesty: he was the person Leontes first confided in when he suspected Hermione of having an affair with Polixenes. It was Camillo who warned Polixenes of Leontes' plan to kill him, and whom

Polixenes asked for help in discovering why Florizel was spending so much time at the shepherd's cottage. Now Florizel appeals to Camillo's sense of righteousness in asking for his help in breaking free of his father. Camillo quickly devises a plan.

'What I do next shall be to tell the King
Of this escape, and whither they are bound'

It is vital to the plot that Camillo remains with Florizel and Perdita after Polixenes has made his threats. We have already been told in Act 4, scene 2 that Camillo wants to return to Sicilia. Now, he cleverly suggests that they flee to Sicilia, where they will be received by the king as a gesture of goodwill. Whilst he is seemingly acting in Florizel's best interests, Camillo admits his true intentions in this aside.

Camillo will tell Polixenes that Florizel and Perdita have gone to the court of Leontes in Sicilia in the hopes that he will insist on following them there. Polixenes had made it clear to Camillo in Act 4, scene 2 that he had no desire to be reconciled with Leontes, as his memory of the tragic events following his last visit still haunt him. When Camillo expressed his wish to return home, Polixenes replied, 'Of that fatal country Sicilia, prithee speak no more...' However, in his desperation to stop the marriage between his son and Perdita, Polixenes will have no choice but to visit Leontes, thereby giving Camillo the opportunity to return home.

One purpose of this long scene is to balance out the action so far between Sicilia and Bohemia. How is this balance achieved? Why is it important? By the end of this scene all the important characters will be on their way to Sicilia. How does this prepare us for the full resolution of the plot?

Note that throughout much of this scene, Camillo has spoken in verse. However, when he and Florizel speak with Autolycus to engineer the exchange of garments, they speak in prose. Why do they change from verse to prose to speak to Autolycus?

Self-test Questions Act Four

Uncover the plot
Delete two of the three alternatives given, to find the correct plot. Beware possible misconceptions and muddles.

Place/Space/Time announces that fifteen/sixteen/seventeen years have passed since the last scene. In this time Camillo/Leontes/Polixenes has grieved and Clown/Florizel/Mamillius has grown into a young man. Emilia/Hermione/Perdita has also grown up and the play will now tell her story. Antigonus/Archidamus/Camillo has served Florizel/Leontes/Polixenes well during these past sixteen days/months/years, but he is now homesick and wants to return to Berlin/

Delphos/Sicilia. Polixenes would rather that he stayed in Bohemia/Capri/Sicilia and help him find out why Clown/Florizel/Mamillius spends so much time at the cottage of a baker/shepherd/woodsman. Both men have heard that the baker/shepherd/woodsman has a beautiful daughter/home/son. Archidamus/Antigonus/Camillo agrees to forget Bohemia/Delphos/Sicilia for the time being and accompany Polixenes, in disguise, to the home of the pedlar/Oracle/shepherd.

Autolycus/Doricles/Shepherd is a travelling pedlar and fool/musician/thief. He meets Clown/Florizel/Shepherd on his way to buy provisions for the bird-calling/cattle-milking/sheep-shearing competition. Clown/Florizel/Shepherd tells Autolycus/Camillo/Antony about the competition. Autolycus/Camillo/Polixenes steals Clown/Florizel/Shepherd's purse and decides to attend the sheep-shearing competition in order to do more sheep-shearing/singing/thieving. Hermione/Paulina/Perdita is lady/queen/princess of the sheep-shearing competition and feast. She welcomes all the guests/musicians/sheep. Two of the guests are Autolycus/Camillo/Leontes and Polixenes in disguise. Both men remark on Hermione/Paulina/Perdita's beauty and common/noble/simple demeanour. A dance/masque/play is performed by the shepherds and shepherdesses. Perdita and Autolycus/Clown/Florizel take part. At the feast, Autolycus/Clown/Florizel calls himself Dorca/Doricles/Mopsa. Autolycus/David/Rosalind arrives, peddling goods and singing songs. A dance/masque/song called 'The Twelve Satyrs' is performed for entertainment. Autolycus/Clown/Florizel tells a disguised Polixenes that he wants to marry Emilia/Mopsa/Perdita, adding that he has reasons for not telling his brother/father/mother about his engagement. Furious/happy/pleased, Polixenes reveals his true identity and asks/encourages/forbids Florizel from ever seeing Hermione/Leontes/Perdita again. Camillo/Polixenes/Shepherd tells Perdita that she will suffer a cruel death/injury/torture if she ever tries to see Autolycus/Banquo/Florizel again.

After his brother's/father's/mother's departure, Antony/Camillo/Florizel declares that he will reject his claim to the throne of Bohemia/Delphos/Sicilia in favour of marrying Perdita. Camillo suggests that they go to Delphos/Rome/Sicilia. Florizel exchanges clothes with Autolycus/Clown/Camillo. Clown and Shepherd are frightened/happy/pleased by Autolycus'/Camillo's/Polixenes' threats and decide to show him the documents about Autolycus'/Doricles'/Perdita's real identity. On their way, they meet Autolycus. As he is dressed in Camillo's/Florizel's/Polixenes' clothes, they believe him to be a courtier/pedlar/thief. He tells them that Florizel/Perdita/Polixenes is on a ship and leads them there.

Who? What? Why? When? Where? How?
1   When does Polixenes reveal his identity to Florizel?
2   What worries Polixenes?
3   What does Florizel call himself at the sheep-shearing contest?
4   Who was born under the influence of Mercury?
5   Why does Autolycus tell Clown and Shepherd that Polixenes is on the ship sailing to Sicilia?
6   How many years have passed since the last scene?
7   How is Autolycus able to convince Clown and Shepherd that he is a courtier?
8   Why does Camillo want to return to Sicilia?
9   Where does Camillo suggest that Florizel and Perdita flee?
10 Why does Autolycus want to attend the sheep-shearing contest?

Who said that, and to whom?
1   'There is no other way but to tell the King she's a changeling,'
2   '...offer me no money, I pray you; that kills my heart.'
3   'He has his health, and ampler strength indeed than most have of his age.'

4 'Some call him Autolycus.'
5 'I should leave grazing, were I of your flock, and only live by gazing.'
6 '...a man, they say, that from very nothing, and beyond the imagination of his neighbours, is grown into an unspeakable estate.'
7 'Even now I tremble to think your father by some accident should pass this way, as you did'
8 'It is fifteen years since I saw my country'
9 'I told you what would come of this.'
10 '...so turtles pair that never mean to part.'

Open quotes
Identify the scene; complete the phrase; identify the speaker and the character being spoken to.
1 '...we marry a gentler scion to the wildest stock...'
2 'Your purse is not hot enough to purchase your spice.'
3 'Thou, a scepter's heir...'
4 'Shepherdess-a fair one are you...'
5 'The King is not at the palace...'
6 'A shepherd's daughter, and what to her adheres...'
7 'We are not furnished like Bohemia's son...'
8 'Prithee be my present partner in this business...'
9 '...in whose company I shall re-view Sicilia...'
10 'She is as forward of her breeding as...'

Act 5, scene 1

At the court of Leontes, Cleomenes and Dion are trying to persuade Leontes to stop his grieving and marry again. He says that he will never be able to replace Hermione. Paulina supports his decision not to marry again. A servant announces the arrival of Florizel, Prince of Bohemia, and his wife. Leontes is shocked that he should be given no forewarning of such a visit. Florizel says that he has been sent by his father, who is too old to make the journey himself. He introduces Perdita as the Princess of Libya. Leontes' welcome is interrupted by the arrival of a lord of Bohemia, who brings Leontes orders from Polixenes to arrest Florizel for running off with a shepherdess. He says that Polixenes is in Sicilia and on his way to the court. Polixenes has also met the shepherdess' father and brother in Sicilia. Florizel knows at once that Camillo has betrayed him. Florizel and Perdita admit to Leontes that they are not yet married. He takes pity on them and promises to speak to Polixenes.

'Do as the heavens have done; forget your evil; With them forgive yourself.'

Forgiveness

As Time told us at the start of Act 4, Leontes has spent these sixteen years grieving. We were told earlier that he has reconciled himself formally with Bohemia, and here we see his own courtiers forgiving him the damage he caused. Whilst Paulina discourages him from marrying again, she has remained a faithful servant to him throughout these sixteen years. She respects him, but feels that it is important that he does not forget that he is responsible for Hermione's death. She mentions her husband's death (indirectly caused by Leontes) but she does not seem bitter. Do you think Leontes forgives himself?

Following this conversation, Florizel and Perdita arrive at Leontes' court. Cleomenes claims that the heavens have forgiven Leontes, and Paulina has reminded them all of the Oracle's judgement, that Leontes should not have an heir until the lost child is found. When Leontes meets Perdita, he remarks on her beauty but has no idea how true Cleomenes' words are or that he is now reunited with his lost child.

The Elizabethans had a strong belief in God's powers of retribution and benevolence. The reuniting of Leontes with his lost daughter would indicate that Leontes has been forgiven by God for his sin. No doubt it is his heartfelt grieving for sixteen years which has earned him God's forgiveness. In what ways did Cleomenes mean that the heavens have forgiven Leontes?

'Will you swear never to marry, but by my free leave?'

Paulina

Like the heavens, Paulina is preparing to forgive Leontes fully. She has no doubt been moved that he has kept to his word and dedicated his life to grieving for his dead wife and son. In this scene, it appears that she is putting him to the final test in convincing him that he should never marry again, despite Dion and Cleomenes' coaxing. Leontes agrees with Paulina that he will never find another wife like Hermione and therefore will never remarry. Once he has given his word, she asks him to swear that he will never remarry unless she chooses his wife. He does as she asks and she says that she will look for a queen for him: '... not be so young as your former, but she shall be such as, walked your first queen's ghost...'. Paulina's words are preparing the audience for the reappearance of Hermione, alive and well. Why do you think Paulina has waited sixteen years to reunite Hermione and Leontes?

'As every present time doth boast itself
Above a better, gone, so must thy grave
Give way to what's seen now.'

Hermione

The servant announcing the arrival of Florizel and Perdita describes the princess as 'the most peerless piece of earth... that e'er the sun shone bright on.' At the mention of rare beauty, Paulina immediately thinks of Hermione in her prime. She addresses Hermione's spirit, explaining the cycle of life that every generation has to give way to the next. Ironically, Perdita inherited her beauty from Hermione. In what ways does Perdita's arrival in Sicilia prepare us for her mother's return?

**'Your honour not o'erthrown by your desires,
I am friend to them and you; upon which errand
I now go toward him.'**

During these sixteen years Leontes has truly changed from his former irrational

Leontes

and jealous self. In this scene he admits Paulina's charge that he killed his wife, asking only that he is seldom reminded of the fact. His own heart probably could not bear his thinking about it constantly. He is genuinely happy for Florizel and Perdita and, when Florizel appeals to him to speak to Polixenes in favour of his marriage, Leontes agrees. Why should he do so? Florizel had lied to him about his reason for coming to the court, Perdita's identity and about their being married. Moreover, Leontes has not seen his friend for sixteen years. Surely he would not want to jeopardise their first meeting by taking sides against Polixenes in family matters?

Act 5, scene 2

Autolycus asks some gentlemen if they know what happened at the court. They tell him of the revelation of Shepherd's documents, revealing that Perdita is the lost Princess of Sicilia, and go on to describe the emotional reconciliation of the kings. The court learned from Clown that Antigonus was eaten by a bear and that the ship which had carried Antigonus and Perdita to Bohemia was wrecked in a storm. Paulina's emotions are mixed, between grief for her husband and joy at the return of the princess. Before they depart, the gentlemen tell of the imminent unveiling of a statue of Hermione. Autolycus thinks about the part he played in these events and meets Clown and Shepherd, who are rejoicing in their new-found status as gentlemen, as deemed by the kings. They forgive Autolycus for thieving from them and agree to speak on his behalf to the prince. All three set off to see the statue.

'the majesty of the creature, in resemblance of the mother'

Once the documents reveal Perdita to be the lost princess, her resemblance

Time and rebirth

to the queen is noticed. Hermione's beauty and gentleness are reborn in her daughter, who will one day go on to be a gracious and much loved Queen of Sicilia. Perdita's beauty was compared to Hermione's in the previous scene, but why was the resemblance not noticed then?

The action in this scene is communicated by way of a third person narrative. Why has Shakespeare chosen to present the revelations by a third party and not first-hand as they happened? What are the advantages of reporting the information in this way? Note, too, that the gentlemen speak in prose, not verse. Look back at Act 1, scene 1 to find out why prose is more suitable in this situation than verse.

'But oh, the noble combat, that 'twixt joy and sorrow was fought in Paulina.'

Paulina

Neither Antigonus nor the ship ever returned from the expedition to abandon the child and Paulina had assumed that they were all lost together. Finally, she hears the truth of her husband's demise. List all the mixed feelings she would be experiencing upon hearing that Perdita grew up safely, while her husband perished in a gruesome death. Look once again at the report of Antigonus' death to the court. Notice how concisely Shakespeare gives relevant details so that we are sure it was Antigonus and not just a nobleman whom Clown witnessed being mauled by the bear. In terms of the plot, Paulina now knows for certain that she is a widow and free to remarry. Review why it was necessary that Antigonus perished.

'If all the world could have seen't, the woe had been universal.'

After being reacquainted with his lost daughter, Leontes has to tell her of the manner of her mother's death, and no doubt how she herself came to be abandoned. Consider how Perdita reacted to this news. Paulina's steward, who is reporting the scene to Autolycus and the other gentlemen, describes Perdita

Repentance

as being 'wounded' by the information. The court responds to her misery with collective grieving.

The shedding of tears in literature is often referred to as cathartic, in that it purges sin. If we view this mass shedding of tears for Hermione as the court's repentance for her death, in what ways is it also cathartic?

'I humbly beseech you, sir, to pardon me all the faults I have committed to your worship'

There are many pleas for forgiveness in this scene. Leontes asks for Polixenes'

Forgiveness

forgiveness for his jealous accusations sixteen years before, and he also asks for forgiveness from Perdita for abandoning her and indirectly causing the deaths of her mother and brother. Polixenes requests Florizel's and Perdita's forgiveness for the threats he made to them over their love affair. Camillo would also wish Florizel's forgiveness in betraying his plans to Polixenes. Many tears are reported to have been shed at the court that day, not just by the characters involved, but by anyone witnessing the reconciliation.

The pleas for forgiveness at the court are echoed in the second half of this scene by Autolycus asking Clown's forgiveness for thieving from him. He even desires the Prince's forgiveness. How is Autolycus' request comical? Why has Shakespeare contrasted the depth of emotion of the first half of the scene with the comical aspirations of Autolycus, Clown and Shepherd?

Act 5, scene 3

The court of Sicilia and visiting court of Bohemia are at Paulina's house for the unveiling of the statue of Hermione. Leontes thanks Paulina for her faithful service these sixteen years. He mentions that Perdita is especially curious to see what her mother looked like. The statue is revealed and everyone falls silent. Leontes, the first to speak, notices that the statue has more wrinkles than Hermione. Leontes and Polixenes comment on how lifelike it is, that it almost appears to be breathing. Paulina then announces that she can make the statue move, and Hermione steps down off the statue base. She has managed to survive all these years by the hope that the Oracle would be fulfilled and that her lost child would be found.

Paulina announces her retirement from courtly duties. Leontes insists that Paulina marry Camillo, as he himself is now reunited with his wife. He reacquaints Hermione with Polixenes and asks for their pardons for his ill behaviour sixteen years before. They leave the chapel in Paulina's house to celebrate the marriages of Florizel to Perdita and Camillo to Paulina.

'I am sorry, sir, I have thus far stirred you; but I could afflict you farther.'

Leontes

Leontes reaches the climax of his repentance in this scene. His very soul is gradually moved to an intensity it had not known before by the image of Hermione. Examine the gradual build-up to the point where the statue moves. Perdita stands beside the statue, reinforcing the resemblance between the living daughter and the image of the mother, one natural and one seemingly artificial. There is much colour in the statue, as if blood is running through its veins, and it appears to breathe. Paulina is purposely stirring Leontes to a state where he will believe that his repentance for his tyranny towards Hermione is willing her back to life. She embellishes the moment of Hermione's 'coming back to life' by calling for music.

The discovery of Perdita's identity is reported through third person narration in order to save the reconciliation of mother, father and daughter for the climax of the final scene. How is this scene more climactic than the preceding one? Why is bringing Hermione back to life more important than the return of the lost daughter?

'Knowing by Paulina that the oracle Gave hope thou wast in being, have preserved Myself to see the issue.'

Hermione

Shakespeare has skilfully prepared us for the revelation that Hermione is indeed alive. Firstly, in Act 5, scene 1, Paulina persuades Leontes not to remarry unless she selects a wife for him. Did you ask yourself at that time why she said this? What were her motives, beyond preserving Hermione's memory? Perhaps you thought that she wished Leontes never to forget his cruelty towards Hermione.

Paulina

In scene 2 of Act 5, the second gentleman observed, 'I thought she (Paulina) had some great matter there in hand, for she hath privately, twice or thrice a day, ever since the death of Hermione, visited that removed house'. Paulina has obviously been attending to Hermione all these years. Were you surprised that Hermione was not dead? Look back at Act 3, scene 2, to Paulina's report of Hermione's apparent death. Paulina says, 'I say she's dead; I'll swear't'. How are her words ambiguous? The suspense is further built up in this scene with the details of the statue's strangely lifelike qualities – its numerous wrinkles, its moving eyes, and the fact that it seems to breathe.

We now have to wonder why Paulina has kept Hermione's survival a secret for sixteen years. Firstly, Hermione was in fact very close to death when she collapsed in the courtroom: the shock of Mamillius' death almost killed her. At the time, Paulina probably felt that for Hermione's safety it was best if Leontes believed her to be dead. He does return to his senses after he is told Mamillius and Hermione are dead. Would he have done so if he had known Hermione was alive? We can only speculate.

Repentance

Paulina's strong sense of morality would tell her that Leontes should repent for his sins. She would not dare tell him the truth about Hermione until she was satisfied that he had truly atoned for his wrongdoing. Why was it crucial to Paulina that Leontes agreed not to remarry without her consent?

It is possible, of course, that Hermione may not have wished to see Leontes during all this time. It was only the hope that the Oracle was correct that gave her the will to live, as she desired more than anything in the world to see her daughter again. Note that Paulina mentions the Oracle to Leontes and the other lords in Act 5, scene 1. Paulina seems to have borne the prophecy in mind more than Leontes. She would have told Hermione that Perdita had returned to Sicilia. Paulina arranges for the court to see the statue of Hermione immediately after learning of Perdita's true identity, but before she has a chance to tell Hermione. Perhaps she was moved to suggest the viewing of the statue so that mother and daughter could see one another. Bearing this in mind, think again about the report of Paulina's reaction to the revelations at the court in Act 5, scene 2. Paulina may have left it up to Hermione to decide whether to forgive Leontes and make the truth of her survival known. Do you think that there is enough evidence, prior to Perdita's identity being revealed, to suggest that Hermione and Leontes would have been reunited if their daughter had not been found?

'For him, I partly know his mind, to find thee An honourable husband.'

Camillo

Paulina

Shakespearean comedies and romances end in multiple marriages, whereas the tragedies end in multiple deaths. The first engagement has been in development since we met Florizel and Perdita in Act 4, scene 4. They were finally given Polixenes' consent when Perdita's true identity was revealed. The reconciliation of Hermione and Leontes is a renewal of vows rather than a new marriage, but nevertheless they reinforce the supremacy of romantic love at the end of the play. The third couple is created in Leontes' closing speech. Camillo and Paulina have each served Leontes well, and indeed, Paulina took over as Leontes' confidant when Camillo fled to Bohemia. Camillo reinforced his loyalty of character in serving Polixenes well for sixteen years. How does Shakespeare prepare Paulina for taking a new husband, and in what ways are Paulina and Camillo well suited to one another?

'Lead us from hence, where we may leisurely Each one demand and answer to his part'

The theme of rebirth predominates in the second half of the play. In this final

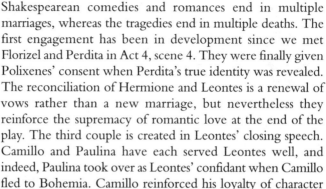

Time and rebirth

scene, Perdita is 'reborn' for Hermione and Hermione is 'reborn' for the court of Sicilia. Now that Leontes and his wife are reconciled, their marriage is 'reborn', as love is 'reborn' for Paulina in her impending marriage to Camillo. Most importantly, happiness and order are 'reborn' for Sicilia, in the reconciliation of their king and queen and the marriage of the future king and queen. Leontes suggests in these lines that they all have a lot of questions to ask one another about the sixteen year interim. List all the questions the characters would want to ask one another. For instance, Hermione and Leontes will want to know about Perdita's upbringing, and Camillo will want to know the chain of events which took place after his departure, leading to the 'death' of Hermione.

The play's title makes reference to the seasons. There are references to the seasons throughout the play and earlier in this act, Camillo mentioned the passing of sixteen summers. The cycle of the four seasons naturally enforces the ideas of time passing and rebirth. Why do you think Shakespeare chose the season of winter for the title? The seasonal cycle is timeless, in that spring will always follow winter and so forth. In what ways are the themes of *The Winter's Tale* timeless?

Leontes' lines above suggest that life has come full circle and that relationships are finally restored to the condition they were in before his jealous episode. Do you think that the reconciled relationships are the same, better or worse? Give your reasons.

Self-test Questions Act Five

Uncover the plot
Delete two of the three alternatives given, to find the correct plot. Beware possible misconceptions and muddles.

Dion and Antigonus/Cleomenes/Camillo tell Leontes he has apologised/grieved/prayed for long enough and deserves to die/go on holiday/remarry. They also suggest that he should have more children/fun/land. Emilia/Paulina/Perdita reminds them of the judgement of Apollo/Athena/Zeus, which said that Leontes would have no heir until his lost child/document/wife is found. Florizel/Leontes/Polixenes says that he will have no other child/lord/wife unless Emilia/Paulina/Perdita chooses one for him. Camillo/Florizel/Richard arrives with his new bride, whom he says is from Albania/Greece/Libya. He says that he has been sent by his country/father/wife as his brother/father/uncle is too ill/old/young to make the trip himself. A message from Camillo/Polixenes/Shepherd arrives. It is an order to detain/dismiss/entertain Florizel, who has betrayed his duty and run off with a milkmaid/seamstress/shepherdess. Dion/Cleomenes/Florizel asks Camillo/Leontes/Paulina to speak to his father on his behalf.

Autolycus/Clown/Shepherd is outside the palace and asks some gentlemen what has happened at the court/festival/trial. They report the revelation of Emilia's/Paulina's/Perdita's true identity. Leontes and Camillo/Florizel/Polixenes are reunited and Leontes asks for Polixenes' address/blessing/forgiveness. Clown/Florizel/Shepherd describes Antigonus'/Camillo's/Cleomenes' violent death, being torn apart by a bear/lion/shark, and the wreck of Leontes' ship. Emilia/Paulina/Perdita does not know whether to be happy at the lost daughter/son/wife being found or sad at the death/injury/sickness of her husband. When Florizel/Leontes/Polixenes tells Perdita about her mother's accident/death/illness, the entire court rejoices/shrieks/sorrows. All of the courtiers go off to see the christening/signing/unveiling of the drawing/painting/statue of Hermione. Autolycus recognises Clown and Florizel/Perdita/Shepherd when they pass by. For their part in revealing Perdita's true identity, they have been made gentlemen/knights/princes. Clown condemns/forgives/reprimands Autolycus for stealing from him and agrees to talk to the king/prince/princess on his behalf.

The court of Sicilia and the visiting court of Bohemia/Greece/Libya go to Emilia's/Paulina's/Perdita's house for the unveiling of the painting/sculpture/statue. Camillo/Leontes/Polixenes thanks Paulina for her sixteen years of loyal grieving/marriage/service. She reveals the statue and Camillo/Leontes/Polixenes remarks that it has more hair/teeth/wrinkles than Antigonus/Hermione/Mamillius had. Leontes and Camillo/Perdita/Polixenes remark on some lifelike features of the statue: it appears to be blinking/breathing/moving. Paulina says that she can make the statue move/sing/talk. Hermione steps down and embraces Leontes/Perdita/Polixenes. She says that the hope of the Oracle/prophet/soothsayer coming true gave her the will to live, so that she might see her daughter/husband/

son again. Camillo/Cleomenes/Paulina announces his/her/their retirement from courtly service. Leontes tells Emilia/Paulina/Perdita to marry Antony/Camillo/Dion. They leave Paulina's house to celebrate the return of Hermione and the two/three/four marriages.

Who? What? Why? When? Where? How?

1 As whose daughter does Florizel introduce Perdita to Leontes' court?
2 Who reputedly sculpted the statue of Hermione?
3 Where has Hermione been living these sixteen years?
4 Who was within a month of the age of Mamillius?
5 Why are the identity documents Shepherd presents to the court believed?
6 How is it slowly revealed that Hermione is actually alive?
7 What reason does Florizel give Leontes for his visit?
8 What items of Antigonus' does Clown reveal to Paulina?
9 What gave Hermione the will to live?
10 Who discourages Leontes from remarrying?

Who said that, and to whom?

1 'Your father's image is so hit in you'
2 'Where hast thou been preserved?'
3 'We shall not marry till thou bidd'st us.'
4 '...thou art as honest a true fellow as any is in Bohemia.'
5 '...there was not full a month between their births.'
6 'Both your pardons, that e'er I put between your holy looks my ill suspicion.'
7 '...at your request my father will grant precious things as trifles.'
8 'I am past more children; but thy sons and daughters will be all gentlemen born.'
9 '... 'tis strange, he should thus steal upon us.'
10 'Hermione was not so much wrinkled, nothing so aged as this seems.'

Open Quotes

Identify the scene; complete the phrase; identify the speaker and the character being spoken to.

1 'Women will love her that she is a woman more worth than any man...'
2 'She had one eye declined for the loss of her husband...'
3 'Thou shouldst a husband take by my consent...'
4 'We are not, sir...'
5 'If all the world could have seen 't...'
6 'I like your silence...'
7 'Whilst I remember her and her virtues...'
8 '...they were to be known by garment...'
9 'I did not well...'
10 'Desires you to attach his son...'

Self-test Answers Act One

Uncover the plot

Polixenes, king of Bohemia, has been visiting Leontes in Sicilia for nine months. Archidamus, Lord of Bohemia, discusses Camillo's possible visit to Bohemia in the summer. Archidamus remarks on the promise shown by Mamillius, son of Leontes. Polixenes is anxious about the state of his kingdom during his absence and decides to return to Bohemia. Leontes cannot convince Polixenes to stay, but Hermione is successful. She tells Polixenes that he must stay either as her guest or prisoner. Leontes has a sudden fit of jealousy, suspecting Polixenes and Hermione are lovers. Leontes starts behaving irrationally and asks Camillo if he knew about the affair between Hermione and Polixenes. Leontes orders Camillo to poison Polixenes. Camillo agrees, although he is convinced Hermione and Polixenes are innocent. Camillo tells Polixenes of Leontes' plan. Camillo and Polixenes plan to leave Sicilia immediately.

Who? What? Why? When? Where? How?

1   One more week
2   He has command of the city gates
3   To avoid a royal scandal and preserve Hermione's honour
4   In the garden
5   Polixenes has been visiting Leontes for nine months
6   A man whose wife has been unfaithful to him
7   Camillo's senses would be dulled so that he would not notice that Bohemia's hospitality is inferior
8   Fears that Mamillius might not be his son
9   Jesus' betrayal by Judas
10 She is to tell him that she is sure all is well in Bohemia

Who said that, and to whom?

1   Hermione to Leontes, explaining that women can be persuaded by praise more easily than by force, Act 1, scene 2
2   Camillo to Polixenes, when agreeing to help him escape from Sicilia, Act 1, scene 2
3   Leontes to Camillo, expressing his desire to kill Polixenes, Act 1, scene 2
4   Leontes to Mamillius, Pollinates and Hermione, commenting on the resemblance between himself and his son, Act 1, scene 2
5   Camillo to Archidamus, describing Leontes' and Polixenes' relationship, Act 1, scene 1
6   Polixenes to Leontes and Hermione, in response to Leontes' question as to whether Polixenes is fond of his son, Act 1, scene 2
7   Polixenes to Hermione, describing his youth with Leontes, Act 1, scene 2
8   Camillo to Leontes, jumping to the conclusion that he has angered Leontes, Act 1, scene 2
9   Polixenes to Camillo, questioning him about the change in Leontes' behaviour, Act 1, scene 2
10 Leontes to himself, at the start of his jealous rage, Act 1, scene 2

Open quotes

1   'that did frisk I' th' sun,' Polixenes describing his boyhood with Leontes. Act 1, scene 2
2   'and my name be yoked with his, that did betray the Best!' Polixenes to Camillo in reaction to hearing that Leontes believes he has touched Hermione.

Act 1, scene 2

3 'and betimes, for 'tis most dangerous.' Camillo warning Leontes about the destructive power of jealousy. Act 1, scene 2

4 'Though you perceive me not how I give line.' Leontes in an aside to himself as he spies on Hermione and Polixenes in the garden. Act 1, scene 2

5 'desire yet their life to see him a man.' Camillo describing to Archidamus how much the Sicilian people love Mamillius. Act 1, scene 1

6 'and the entreaties of our most gracious mistress.' Camillo in response to Leontes' question as to why Polixenes has decided to extent his visit. Act 1, scene 2

7 'but I, though you would seek t'unsphere the stars with oaths, should yet say, "Sir, no going."' Hermione persuading Polixenes to stay. Act 1, scene 2

8 'without my present vengeance taken;' Camillo in response to Leontes' charge that Hermione has committed adultery. Act 1, scene 2

9 'Which shows me mine changed too:' Polixenes persuading Camillo to tell him the truth about the change in Leontes' behaviour. Act 1, scene 2

10 'Its tenderness, and make itself a pastime to harder bosoms!' Leontes speaking cryptically to Polixenes, Mamillius and Hermione about how tenderness can lead to lust. Act 1, scene 2

Self-test Answers Act Two

Uncover the plot

Hermione and her ladies-in-waiting are being entertained by Mamillius. Hermione asks Mamillius to tell a tale. He says that a sad tale is best for winter. They are interrupted by the arrival of Leontes and his lords. He has just learned of the secret departure of Polixenes and Camillo. Leontes believes that Camillo's betrayal of his orders proves more strongly that Polixenes is guilty. Leontes publicly humiliates Hermione. He says she has been unfaithful and orders her to prison. She reacts bravely to her imprisonment. Antigonus defends Hermione's innocence. Antigonus says that if Hermione is guilty of adultery, then he will keep his own wife attached to him by a leash. To prove that his judgement is right, Leontes has sent two lords to the Oracle at Delphos.

Paulina, wife of Antigonus, tries to visit Hermione. The jailer has orders not to permit anyone to visit the queen. She is able to see Emilia, an attendant to the queen. Emilia tells her that the queen has given birth. Paulina believes that if Leontes saw the innocence of the baby than he would be moved to retract his accusation against Hermione and return to his senses.

Leontes cannot sleep. He will find no peace until Hermione is punished. Paulina shows him the baby. He calls it a bastard and orders it to be burned. He calls his lords traitors, but they say that burning the child to death is too cruel and will have terrible consequences. Leontes instead orders the child to be abandoned. Dion and Cleomenes return from Delphos. Leontes calls for a public trial for Hermione.

Who? What? Why? When? Where? How?

1 Polixenes, Camillo and Hermione

2 Leontes, Hermione and Mamillius will suffer terrible consequences

3 They have been gone twenty-three days

4 She never considers that Leontes might reject his daughter, believing her to be fathered by Polixenes

5 At Delphos in Greece
6 A strange deserted country
7 She says that the baby was born free and is not involved in Leontes' charges against Hermione
8 The stress of her imprisonment and her public humiliation by her husband
9 He is obsessed with punishing Hermione
10 She is innocent, but it is God's will that she is sent to prison and she must accept God's will

Who said that, and to whom?
1 Leontes to Paulina and Antigonus about his children, whom he believes to be bastards, in Act 2, scene 3
2 Antigonus defending Hermione to Leontes, in Act 2, scene 1
3 Paulina telling the servant that she must see Leontes to put his mind at rest once he is shown his new daughter, in Act 2, scene 3
4 Jailer to Paulina, in Act 2, scene 2
5 Mamillius to Hermione and her ladies-in-waiting, in Act 2, scene 1
6 Leontes to the lords and attendants, in Act 2, scene 3
7 Leontes in dismissing Antigonus' defence of Hermione, in Act 2, scene 1
8 Emilia reporting to Paulina what Hermione says to her baby, in Act 2, scene 2
9 Paulina to Leontes, in Act 2, scene 3
10 Leontes to the court about Camillo's defection to Polixenes, Act 2, scene 1

Open Quotes
1 'Not she which burns in't.' Paulina's response to Leontes' threat to have her burned. Act 2, scene 3
2 'Away with her to prison.' Leontes to the court on publicly announcing Hermione's adultery. Act 2, scene 1
3 'say that she were gone, given to the fire, a moiety of my rest might come to me again.' Leontes to his attendants about not being able to rest until Hermione has been punished. Act 2, scene 3
4 'let't not be doubted I shall do good.' Paulina to Emilia hoping that her plan will be successful. Act 2, scene 2
5 'I have one of sprites and goblins.' Mamillius to Hermione and her ladies-in-waiting in response to Hermione's request to Mamillius to tell a tale. Act 2, scene 1
6 'To save the innocent – anything possible.' Antigonus to Leontes about the lengths he would go to save the baby's life. Act 2, scene 3
7 'lest your justice prove violence, in which three great ones suffer, yourself, your queen, your son.' Antigonus warning Leontes of the consequences of his judgement if it is wrong. Act 2, scene 1
8 'As passes colouring.' Paulina to herself in reaction to the jailer having to be present during her meeting with Emilia. Act 2, scene 2
9 'to be thy nurses! Wolves and bears, they say, casting their savageness aside, have done   like offices of pity.' Antigonus to Leontes about the chances of the baby's survival. Act 2, scene 3
10 'the want of which vain dew perchance shall dry your pities.' Hermione to Leontes and the court, after she has been ordered to prison. Act 2, scene 1

Self-test Answers Act Three

Uncover the plot

Cleomenes remarks on the beauty of the island of Delphos, while Dion describes the pomp and ceremony of the Oracle. Cleomenes asks Apollo to end Hermione's suffering.

Leontes opens the proceedings at the court of justice. Hermione is charged with high treason in committing adultery with Polixenes, conspiring to kill Leontes and helping Camillo and Polixenes to escape. Hermione pleads not guilty and says that she is fighting for her honour. Leontes tells her that he has cast out the baby. Hermione calls for the Oracle to be read out. The Oracle finds Hermione chaste, Polixenes blameless and Camillo a true subject. Leontes is found to be a jealous tyrant who rejects the Oracle's judgement. A servant announces that Mamillius has died, and Hermione faints. Paulina scolds Leontes harshly for his tyrannical behaviour. He says that he accepts her judgement. His nobility returns and he says that he will visit Hermione's and Mamillius' graves every day.

Antigonus arrives on the coast of Bohemia, where a storm is threatening. He has had a terrible dream. Hermione warned him that if he carries out Leontes' orders then he will never see Paulina again. He follows the orders because he believes that Perdita is illegitimate. On his way back to the ship he is pursued and half eaten by a bear. Shepherd finds Perdita whilst his son Clown witnesses the shipwreck and Antigonus' death. They believe the baby was left as a gift by fairies, so that they must keep it a secret. Shepherd takes the baby home.

Who? What? Why? When? Where? How?

1   Five – his wife, his son, his daughter, his friend and his loyal servant
2   He died from thoughts and fears over his mother's fate
3   They are travelling on horseback
4   Mourning the deaths of Hermione and Mamillius
5   A remote part of Bohemia
6   Her father is the Emperor of Russia
7   The voice sounded like thunder
8   The murder of an innocent Polixenes
9   They may lose the gift they have been given by the fairies
10 When the baby is found

Who said that, and to whom?

1   The mariner to Antigonus about the storm brewing, in Act 3, scene 3
2   Hermione to Leontes in Act 3, scene 2
3   Hermione to the court of justice, in Act 3, scene 2
4   Leontes to Paulina about how he will mourn the deaths of his wife and son, in Act 3, scene 2
5   The mariner to Antigonus about the dangerous creatures of this remote part of Bohemia, in Act 3, scene 3
6   Hermione to Leontes in her final speech on the stand before the Oracle is read, in Act 3, scene 2
7   Dion to Cleomenes about the ceremony of the Oracle in Act 3, scene 1
8   Paulina to Leontes assuming that he will punish her too, in Act 3, scene 2
9   Shepherd to Clown about their luck in finding Perdita, in Act 3, Scene 3
10 Leontes to Paulina after Mamillius has died and Hermione has fainted, in Act 3, scene 2

1   'And still rest thine.' Antigonus hoping that the gold left with Perdita will last her through her upbringing and adulthood. Act 3, scene 3
2   'if that which is lost be none found.' Officer reading the Oracle's judgement to the court of justice. Act 3, scene 2
3   'and Tyranny Tremble at Patience.' Hermione to the court of justice, after pleading not guilty. Act 3, scene 2
4   'I have deserved all tongues to talk their bitt'rest.' Leontes agreeing with Paulina that he did behave like a tyrant. Act 3, scene 2
5   'and we'll do good deeds on 't.' Shepherd to Clown about their lucky find. Act 3, scene 3
6   'this is mere falsehood.' Leontes rejecting the Oracle's judgement. Act 3, scene 2
7   'the temple much surpassing the common praise it bears.' Cleomenes to Dion about the island of Delphos and the Oracle there, Act 3, scene 1
8   'could not move the gods to look that way thou wert.' Paulina to Leontes about the evil he has done. Act 3, scene 2
9   'and most accursed am I to be by oath enjoined to this.' Antigonus after he has abandoned Perdita. Act 3, scene 3
10 'Does my deeds make the blacker!' Leontes about Camillo's innocence and honour. Act 3, scene 2

Self-test Answers Act Four

Uncover the plot

Time announces that sixteen years have passed since the last scene. In this time Leontes has grieved and Florizel has grown into a young man. Perdita has also grown up and the play will now tell her story. Camillo has served Polixenes well during these past sixteen years, but he is now homesick and wants to return to Sicilia. Polixenes would rather that he stayed in Bohemia and help him find out why Florizel spends so much time at the cottage of a shepherd. Both men have heard that the shepherd has a beautiful daughter. Camillo agrees to forget Sicilia for the time being and accompany Polixenes, in disguise, to the home of the shepherd.

Autolycus is a travelling pedlar and thief. He meets Clown on his way to buy provisions for the sheep-shearing competition. Clown tells Autolycus about the competition. Autolycus steals Clown's purse and decides to attend the sheep-shearing competition in order to do more thieving. Perdita is queen of the sheep-shearing competition and feast. She welcomes all the guests. Two of the guests are Camillo and Polixenes in disguise. Both men remark on Perdita's beauty and noble demeanour. A dance is performed by the shepherds and shepherdesses, in which Perdita and Florizel take part. At the feast, Florizel calls himself Doricles. Autolycus arrives, peddling goods and singing songs. A masque called 'The Twelve Satyrs' is performed for entertainment. Florizel tells a disguised Polixenes that he wants to marry Perdita, adding that he has reasons for not telling his father about his engagement. Furious, Polixenes reveals his true identity and bans Florizel from ever seeing Perdita again. Polixenes tells Perdita that she will suffer a cruel death if she ever tries to see Florizel again.

After his father's departure, Florizel declares that he will reject his claim to the throne of Bohemia in favour of marrying Perdita. Camillo suggests that they go to Sicilia. Florizel exchanges clothes with Autolycus. Clown and Shepherd are frightened by Polixenes' threats and decide to show him the documents about Perdita's real identity. On their way, they meet Autolycus. As he is dressed in Florizel's clothes, they believe him to be a courtier. He tells them that Polixenes is on a ship and leads them there.

Who? What? Why? When? Where? How?
1 After Florizel has expressed his desire to marry Perdita
2 Polixenes is worried that Prince Florizel had fallen in love with a peasant girl
3 Florizel calls himself Doricles
4 Autolycus is born under the influence of Mercury
5 Autolycus believes that Florizel will offer him money for keeping Polixenes away
6 Sixteen years have passed
7 He is wearing Florizel's courtly clothing
8 Camillo is homesick for Sicilia and wishes to die there
9 He suggests that they go to Sicilia
10 Autolycus hopes that he will be able to steal money easily from the the simple shepherds at the sheep-shearing contest

Who said that, and to whom?
1 Clown to Shepherd about Perdita's true identity, in Act 4, scene 4
2 Autolycus refusing Clown's offer of money. (He has already stolen Clown's purse so he does not want him to discover it is missing, in Act 4, scene 3)
3 Florizel to the disguised Polixenes about his father, in Act 4, scene 4
4 Autolycus deceiving Clown about who allegedly robbed him, in Act 4, scene 3
5 Camillo to Perdita about her beauty, in Act 4, scene 4
6 Polixenes to Camillo about Shepherd, in Act 4, scene 2
7 Perdita to Florizel over her fear of Polixenes discovering their love affair, in Act 4, scene 4
8 Camillo telling Polixenes of his desire to return to Sicilia, in Act 4, scene 2
9 Perdita to Florizel in reaction to Polixenes' threats, in Act 4, scene 4
10 Florizel to Perdita about the strength of their love, in Act 4, scene 4

Open quotes
1 'And make conceive a bark of baser kind by bud of nobler race.' Polixenes to Perdita about the mixing of wild and cultivated plants. Act 4, scene 4
2 'I'll be with you at your sheep-shearing too;' Autolycus to himself after he has stolen Clown's purse and plans to attend the sheep-shearing contest. Act 4, scene 3
3 'That thus affect'st a sheep-hook!' Polixenes to Florizel forbidding his marriage to Perdita. Act 4, scene 4
4 'well you fit our ages with flow'rs of winter.' Polixenes to Perdita. Act 4, scene 4
5 'he is gone aboard a new ship, to purge melancholy and air himself;' Autolycus lying to Clown and Shepherd about the king's whereabouts. Act 4, scene 4
6 'which follows after, is th' argument of Time.' Time to the audience about the shift in focus from Leontes to Perdita. Act 4, scene 1
7 'Nor shall appear in Sicilia.' Florizel to Camillo about what he and Perdita are wearing to be received at the court of Sicilia. Act 4, scene 4
8 'and lay aside the thoughts of Sicilia.' Polixenes urging Camillo to remain in Bohemia and help him discover what attraction Shepherd's cottage holds for Florizel. Act 4, scene 2
9 'for whose sight I have a woman's longing.' Camillo to himself about his longing to return to Sicilia. Act 4, scene 4
10 'She is I' th' rear 'our birth.' Florizel to Camillo about Perdita's innate grace and nobility. Act 4, scene 4

Self-test Answers Act Five

Uncover the plot

Dion and Cleomenes tell Leontes he has grieved for long enough and deserves to remarry. They also suggest that he should have more children. Paulina reminds them of the judgement of Apollo, which said that Leontes would have no heir until his lost child is found. Leontes says that he will have no other wife unless Paulina chooses one for him. Florizel arrives with his new bride, whom he says is from Libya. He says that he has been sent by his father as his father is too old to make the trip himself. A message from Polixenes arrives. It is an order to detain Florizel, who has betrayed his duty and run off with a shepherdess. Florizel asks Leontes to speak to his father on his behalf.

Autolycus is outside the palace and asks some gentlemen what has happened at the court. They report the revelation of Perdita's true identity. Leontes and Polixenes are reunited and Leontes asks for Polixenes' forgiveness. Clown describes Antigonus' violent death, being torn apart by a bear, and the wreck of Leontes' ship. Paulina does not know whether to be happy at the lost daughter being found or sad at the death of her husband. When Leontes tells Perdita about her mother's death, the entire court sorrows. All the courtiers go off to see the unveiling of the statue of Hermione. Autolycus recognises Clown and Shepherd when they pass by. For their part in revealing Perdita's true identity, they have been made gentlemen. Clown forgives Autolycus for stealing from him and agrees to talk to the prince on his behalf.

The court of Sicilia and the visiting court of Bohemia go to Paulina's house for the unveiling of the statue. Leontes thanks Paulina for her sixteen years of loyal service. She reveals the statue and Leontes remarks that it has more wrinkles than Hermione had. Leontes and Polixenes remark on some lifelike features of the statue: it appears to be breathing. Paulina says that she can make the statue move. Hermione steps down and embraces Leontes. She speaks and says that the hope of the Oracle coming true gave her the will to live, so that she might see her daughter again. Paulina announces her retirement from courtly service. Leontes tells Paulina to marry Camillo. They leave Paulina's house to celebrate the return of Hermione and the two marriages.

Who? What? Why? When? Where? How?

1   The king of Libya
2   Julio Romano
3   Paulina's house
4   Florizel
5   They are written in Antigonus' hand
6   The statue has more wrinkles than Hermione had, it appears to be breathing, the veins have colour in them and her eyes appear to be moving
7   He says that his father, who is too old to make the journey, has sent him
8   He shows Paulina Antigonus' handkerchief and rings
9   The thought of the Oracle being fulfilled
10 Paulina

Who said that, and to whom?

1   Leontes to Florizel about his resemblance to his father, in Act 5, scene 1
2   Hermione asking Perdita where she grew up, in Act 5, scene 3
3   Leontes to Paulina about getting married again, in Act 5, scene 1
4   Clown to Autolycus about what he will say to the Prince on Autolycus' behalf, in Act 5, scene 2

5 Paulina to Leontes about Florizel being the same age as Mamillius, in Act 5, scene 1
6 Leontes asking Polixenes and Hermione to forgive his jealous accusations of sixteen years ago, in Act 5, scene 3
7 Florizel asking Leontes to speak to his father on their behalf, in Act 5, scene 1
8 Shepherd to Clown about their new status as gentlemen, in Act 5, scene 2
9 Leontes to Paulina about the unannounced visit from Florizel, in Act 5, scene 1
10 Leontes' first comment to Paulina about the statue of Hermione, in Act 5, scene 3

Open quotes
1 'men, that she is the rarest of all women.' Servant to Paulina about Perdita's beauty. Act 5, scene 1
2 'another elevated that the oracle was fulfilled.' A gentleman describes Paulina's mixed emotions at the day's revelations. Act 5, scene 2
3 'As I by thine a wife.' Leontes giving Paulina his consent to marry again now that he is reunited with his wife. Act 5, scene 3
4 'nor are we like to be;' Perdita's response to Leontes as to whether she and Florizel are married. Act 5, scene 1
5 'the woe had been universal.' A gentleman describes the mass grief at the court when Perdita learned of her mother's death. Act 5, scene 2
6 'it the more shows off your wonder.' Paulina commenting on the court's silence when the statue is revealed. Act 5, scene 3
7 'I cannot forget my blemishes in them,' Leontes still grieving over Hermione. Act 5, scene 1
8 'not by favor.' A gentleman describes the emotional reconciliation of Polixenes and Leontes. Act 5, scene 2
9 'I meant well.' Paulina's response to Leontes' gratitude for serving him so well. Act 5, scene 3
10 'who has his dignity and duty both cast off…' Polixenes' message to Leontes to detain Florizel. Act 5, scene 1

■ Writing an examination essay

Take the following to heart

- *Carefully study each of the questions set on a particular text* Make sure you understand what they are asking for so that you select the one you know most about.
- *Answer the question* Obvious, isn't it? But bitter experience shows that many students fail because they do not actually answer the question that has been set.
- *Answer all the question* Again, obvious, but so many students spend all their time answering just part of a question and ignoring the rest. This prevents you gaining marks for the parts left out.

The question

1 Read and understand every word of it. If it asks you to compare (the similarities) and/or contrast (the differences) between characters or events, then that is what you must do.
2 Underline all the key words and phrases that mention characters, events and themes, and all instructions as to what to do, e.g. compare, contrast, outline, comment, give an account, write about, show how/what/where.
3 Now write a short list of the things you have to do, one item under the other. A typical question will only have between two and five items at most for you to cope with.

Planning your answer

1 Look at each of the points you have identified from the question. Think about what you are going to say about each. Much of it will be pretty obvious, but if you think of any good ideas, jot them down before you forget them.
2 Decide in what order you are going to deal with the question's major points. Number them in sequence.
3 So far you have done some concentrated, thoughtful reading and written down maybe fifteen to twenty words. You know roughly what you are going to say in response to the question and in what order – if you do not, you have time to give serious thought to trying one of the other questions.

Putting pen to paper

The first sentences are important. Try to summarise your response to the question so the examiner has some idea of how you are going to approach it. Do not say 'I am going to write about the character of Macbeth and show how evil he was' but instead write 'Macbeth was a weak-willed, vicious traitor. Totally dominated by his "fiend-like queen", he deserved the epitaph "this dead butcher" – or did he?' Jump straight into the essay, do not nibble at its extremities for a page and a half. High marks will be gained by the candidate who can show he or she has a mind engaged with the text. Your personal response is rewarded – provided you are answering the question!

As you write your essay *constantly refer back to your list of points* and make sure you are actually responding to them.

How long should it be?

There is no 'correct' length. What you must do is answer the question set, fully and sensitively, in the time allowed. Allocate time to each question according to the percentage of marks awarded for it.

How much quotation or paraphrase?

Use only that which is relevant and contributes to the quality and clarity of your answer. Padding is a waste of your time and gains not a single mark.